The NOT FOR SALE Church

How God brought new life and purpose to a dying urban church

by

William L. Jenkins
and
Anita Cabral

VANDOR

The NOT FOR SALE Church
How God brought new life and purpose to a dying urban church
by William L. Jenkins and Anita Cabral

Printed in the United States of America

ISBN-13: 978-1523701131

Cover image by David Stump Graphics

ChristSD.com
Vandor.com

Table of Contents

Foreword

The United States Census Bureau calculates **more than 4,000 churches close their doors each year**, compared to just over 1,000 new church starts. So the net loss each year is 3,000 churches!

This is the story of one church that did not.

*"If we want things to stay as they are,
things will have to change!"*
"The Leopard" (1963)

Introduction

This is a resurrection story, a tale of how a struggling, dying church found new life and vitality. The model is simple; simple, but not easy. It took a decade of discernment, prayer, sacrifice, toil and tears.

"Christ in the Heart of San Diego" was a 26,000 square-foot building used mostly for an hour on Sunday mornings. Once the largest Evangelical United Brethren Church west of the Rockies, Christ Church had declined from 700 members to an average worship attendance of 40.

Today, Christ Ministry Center (CMC) opens our doors at 6:30 a.m. and closes them at 9:30 p.m. SEVEN DAYS A WEEK! We touch over 1,200 lives every week, offering "abundant help" for spiritual and physical necessities. CMC is completely self-sustaining, with no additional funds from the denomination or grants to operate.

Every church is distinct. While some of the CMC experiences are unique, there are without doubt universal principles we discovered that apply to all churches. The goal of this book is to share the hard learned lessons so other struggling congregations may find their own way to successfully minister with vitality in our fast changing world.

This book offers narratives, tools for discernment and practical assessments to find God's path forward for struggling and declining churches.

This book is not a plan to just keep the lights on and the doors open. A dead-and-dying church that finds a revenue source, but remains dead-and-dying, will inevitably perish. Too many churches have chosen that path. They simply are delaying the inevitable.

Again, this is not a model to simply survive, but to thrive by becoming engaged in God's plan and Christ's model of ministry and service.

In the pages ahead we will seek to answer some of the following dozen questions.

- What is a "Ministry Center"?
- What is the Ministry Center Model?
- Whose church is this, anyway?
- How do we assess if this is for our church?
- How does our church become a Ministry Center?

7

- What are the "potholes" to avoid?
- What are the universal principles?
- How much does it cost?
- What leadership is necessary for success?
- How do we surrender control and win?
- How can church administration be exciting?
- How do you "think abundance" as a Fount of Blessings?

Thank you for joining the journey to vitality.

Prologue

My Journey from Church to Ministry Center

Before beginning the journey from church to Ministry Center, I will tell the story of my own pilgrimage from rural farm boy to urban ministry. I share this, not to call attention to myself, but to illustrate how God can use anyone willing to step out in faith to rethink, revive and revitalize their church, especially an urban church. No one is more surprised that someone from the most non-urban place in America would guide a dying inner city church not only to survive, but thrive. It is all God's doing, not a plan of my own creation. Perhaps telling this story will offer hope and a model for churches facing closure.

At the outset, I want to embrace that this book focuses primarily on urban or suburban churches. However, I am aware of how three small rural churches in Indiana joined together to form their own version of a Ministry Center. They formed a coalition where each church fulfilled a need in their county. One church hosted a food bank. Another provided a clothes closet. The third church offered a place for support groups to meet, dealing with various forms of addictions, grief recovery and family counseling.

The principles discovered at Christ Ministry Center are universal, transcending urban-rural settings, denominational and ethnic diversity.

Humble Beginnings

It's a long way from Yazoo City, Mississippi to San Diego, California. Not just in miles.

Yazoo City sits along the line of demarcation between the Mississippi delta and hills. The four-room shack into which I was born sat right on that borderline at the foot of Graball Hill. Nine of us, my parents, my three brothers and three sisters lived in that house. There was no indoor bathroom, no running water (except the water I ran from the cistern in a five-gallon bucket). Mother cooked our meals on a wood-burning stove. We took a bath every Saturday night, whether we needed it or not, in a round tub that hung on the side of the house the rest of the week. My mother and sisters washed our clothes with a scrub board and ringer washer. I still remember when we got electricity, our first party-line phone, and television.

We grew vegetables and raised chickens and pigs. I do not recall ever being seriously hungry, or worrying about the next meal. While we were definitely poor, there was a childish ignorance of the surrounding poverty. We were rich in the things money cannot buy: family, love and faith.

There were few things I had in common with urban children of my age, except perhaps poverty.

Call to Ministry

Yazoo City had other lines of delineation, some racial and some religious. Baptists were the largest group. We were deep-water Southern Baptists to whom I am grateful for pounding the Bible into my brain. We practically lived at the church. Church was our second home. So it was not surprising I felt a calling into ministry at the very early age of 9.

Education

My parents insisted that each of us get a good education. We all received a quality education in the Yazoo City public schools. Being next to the youngest, there was not much money to send me to college. Thanks to a band scholarship and a weekend job at the radio station, I was able to attend Holmes Junior College. With a couple years' experience, I got a job at a radio station in Cleveland, MS where Delta State is located. I graduated with a double major in education and communication.

During senior year, 1969-70, my student teaching assignment was at Rosedale, an all-Black high school in the heart of the impoverished Mississippi Delta. Most schools in Mississippi were still segregated. Breaking the color barrier at Rosedale set me off upon a lifelong, but slowly evolving, trajectory toward ministry and social justice.

The other major event during college was following through on my childhood call to ministry. As a student pastor I had opportunities to "fill the pulpit" in nearby churches, mostly when the pastor was away on vacation.

One of the churches invited me to preach when their pastor resigned. They invited me back a second week, and then a third week. They invited me to become interim pastor while searching for a full-time pastor. After a couple months, they "called" me to be their permanent "student pastor". In the Baptist church, a person is usually not ordained until receiving a call to become a full time pastor. At age 20, I was ordained a Southern Baptist pastor.

Two components of an unfolding career toward social justice and urban ministry were in place. I was a bi-vocational pastor-teacher. After graduation, I remained at that church a year and taught middle school math.

Louisville: First Taste of Urban Ministry

I was sure God wanted me to attend seminary. Without a job or means of support, it was a huge leap of faith to enroll at Southern Baptist Seminary in Louisville, Kentucky. With so many churches in Kentucky and southern Indiana served by seminarians, the prospects for finding a student pastorate were not promising. Miraculously, a church near Owensboro, a three-hour drive from the seminary, invited me to be their pastor. Many churches in that area did not like the stigma of having a student rather than a full-time pastor. So they permitted me to attend seminary on the condition I return every Wednesday night for prayer meeting. For three years I made two round trips between Owensboro and Louisville each week. It required leaving home at 4:00 a. m. on Tuesdays and Thursdays for my first class.

The first experience of real urban ministry was in Louisville. Southern Seminary required one hour of field education each week. Many of those experiences took me into downtown Louisville to soup kitchens, homeless shelters, and rescue missions. This was boot camp for what was to follow in urban ministry.

Green Bay: First Step to Urban Ministry

After graduation from Southern Seminary in 1974, I accepted the call to a Southern Baptist "home mission" church in Green Bay, Wisconsin. While Green Bay was not a major urban area, it was a major step up from my first two rural student pastorates. During three years in Green Bay, it was necessary to make both personal and ministerial trips to Madison, Milwaukee, Minneapolis and Chicago. God was expanding my knowledge of urban ministry in steps I could absorb.

While serving in Green Bay, I applied for enrollment in the Doctor of Ministry program at Midwestern Baptist Seminary in Kansas City, Missouri, the nearest Baptist seminary. Midwestern was the newest and smallest of the six SBC seminaries, but had taken leadership in developing the Doctor of Ministry (D.Min.) degree program. Most professions had instituted a degree for those who "practice" a profession as opposed to the Doctor of Philosophy (Ph.D.) designed for those who conduct research or teach at a college or university level. There was a great need for an advanced professional degree for ministers who "practice ministry", similar to the Juris Doctor (J.D.) degree for lawyers who "practice law" rather than teach law.

The course of study at Midwestern required a minimum of two years beyond the Master of Divinity (M.Div.) degree. During that time, at least five one-month in-residence seminars were required. Each seminar also required extensive reading in preparation for the seminar and follow up academic papers after the on-campus experience. It was impossible to work all five seminars into two years and serve a full-time pastorate. For most, it was a three to five year course of study. My first seminar was "Mission to Society" in July 1976, America's Bicentennial. It was a game changer, part of God's preparation for urban ministry.

Kansas City: The "Urban Plunge"
If Louisville was boot camp, Kansas City (KC) was full immersion into urban ministry. In July 1976, I spent three days on the streets of Kansas City. It was part of a seminar for the doctoral program at Midwestern. Each doctoral seminarian was required to take the "urban plunge". We had to sign a document releasing Midwestern of liability in case we were killed or died while on the plunge. We had to live as though we were homeless, with nothing more than two quarters and our Social Security cards for identification if that became necessary.

It was extremely hot, 100 degrees in the concrete jungle of downtown KC. Paired off for safety, we were required to rendezvous with our partner every three hours during the day. If our partner did not show up at the appointed place and time, the two quarters were to call the seminary who would notify the police. At night, we were required to stay together, sleeping on park benches or in the grass of a downtown KC park.

We were not allowed to tell anyone the truth and blow our cover. Our task was to survive on the streets for three days using just our wits to see what it is like to be homeless. No showers, no change of clothing, no meals (unless we made the money to buy them) for three long, hot days.

A couple of my buddies were hired as day laborers, washing dishes or yard work. I had the good fortune of sitting next to a delegate to the 1976 National Republican Convention which was in downtown KC at the same time. He asked me how things were going. I gave him my pan-handler hard-luck story without blowing my cover. He must have taken pity, because he handed over a $5 bill. Back then, that was like $25. I had it made and survived three days on cheeseburgers at McDonalds.

From the urban plunge I witnessed what it is like to be homeless, living on the streets. Police treated black vagrants differently than they treated me, a white vagrant. Some people we encountered had been on the streets for years and had lost all hope. Many were just good folks who suffered some misfortune, especially in the devastating OPEC oil embargo economy that led to 18% inflation.

After surviving the plunge, the month long seminar included several other urban training events. We met with city leaders who were involved with KC's "urban renewal project", and met with urban activists, including the leader of the KC Black Panthers. In honesty, I did not plan on becoming an urban minister. Like many of my colleagues, I wanted to someday become pastor of a First Church in a county seat town, the gold standard for success for most Protestant seminarians.

Atlanta: Urban Ministry in Action
After three winters in Green Bay, this Mississippian was ready to return to the sunny South. In 1977, I became Associate Pastor and Minister of Education at Columbia Drive Baptist Church in Decatur, Georgia, a suburb of Atlanta. Dr. J. Don Aderhold, senior pastor, became my mentor. He taught me much, mostly by his example. That is as great a compliment as I can give, for it means he was genuinely a man of God in both word and deed. When I arrived, Don had already served that remarkable congregation 30 years. And he was just getting going.

Don't Cut and Run
The first thing I learned from Don was a lesson in urban ministry: Don't cut and run! Don served during World War II as a Lieutenant, Junior Grade, and was second in command of a submarine combat patrol craft. When Columbia Drive Church organized in 1949, Don became her first, and for almost 50 years, her only pastor. The 1950s were boom years for churches, and Columbia Drive thrived under Don's leadership, building the handsome edifice across the street from Columbia Theological Seminary and down the street from Agnes Scott College and Emory University. Sunday attendance reached 800. But by the time I arrived in 1977, "urban blight and white flight" had begun. Many of the churches closed their doors in fear, sold their property (if they could find buyers) and raced to the new suburbs. That was not so with Don Aderhold and Columbia Drive. His integrity and Navy tenacity would not allow him to cut and run just because his church field was now "red and yellow, black and white". He once told me, "God sent me here to minister to this community, and he hasn't released me from that vow." Yes, attendance and offerings were not

13

what they once were, but the church survived with a wonderful blend of races and cultures.

Embrace Diversity
The second and closely related lesson was about embracing diversity. Only those who grew up in the Deep South fully understand that in 1977, while social changes were slowly taking place, segregation remained firmly entrenched, especially at 11:00 a. m. on Sunday in churches. Don had already led his congregation to welcome the increasingly diverse neighbors; no small feat in Atlanta at that time. Few pastors were willing or able to do that; not then, not there. It was not just a black/white issue. When I arrived, Columbia Drive had become home to over 200 Cambodian (Hmong) refugees from the horrors of Pol Pot's Khmer Rouge massacres and widening Viet Nam communism. Don welcomed the opportunity to nurture and help assimilate these refugees. My first assignment was teaching English as a Second Language (ESL) to the Cambodians with my Mississippi accent, not knowing a word of Cambodian. I learned to love them, and felt their love in return. That was a lesson put into practice years later in San Diego. Even when you don't speak the same language, love transcends the barriers, just as it did at Pentecost.

Be Ecumenical
Thirdly, and on a more personal level, Don taught me about ecumenical ministry. Dr. Aderhold was a scholar. He earned his Doctor of Sacred Theology degree from Columbia Theological Seminary, located right across the street from the church. He taught courses for Columbia. Don suggested that I transfer from Midwestern to Columbia, midway through doctoral studies. But a Baptist minister at a Presbyterian Seminary? It surely had not hindered Don's ministry. So I transferred to Columbia Seminary; one of the best decisions I ever made. Don coached and encouraged me to complete my doctorate at Columbia. My dissertation, written during the infancy of the personal computer revolution, dealt with the use of technology in a church. That was to become the third dimension to my evolving tri-vocational career: ministry, education and technology.

Biloxi: Becoming Methodist
In 1983, I returned to Mississippi. It was as if I needed to return home to get my spiritual bearings reset. Turmoil in the Southern Baptist Convention increased to the point I could no longer with integrity support those who had successfully staged a takeover of the SBC. Many of my most beloved professors at Southern and Midwestern were fired. Black lists were kept on

pastors who, in the opinion of a small group of power brokers, were "too liberal".

In 1988, I made a most difficult decision, resigning the pulpit in Biloxi and leaving the denomination I had loved and served as pastor for 20 years. I wasn't sure I wanted to continue in pastoral ministry at all. By chance, after attending worship at a United Methodist Church, the pastor and I became great friends. He took me under his wing and introduced me to his District Superintendent (DS). Cautious of a former Baptist pastor, the DS invited me to preach at a small two-church charge in Hancock County, Mississippi, near New Orleans. Here in this quiet place I found peace and healing for my soul and spirit. Here I discovered I had been a Methodist all along, immediately identifying with John Wesley's equilibrium of evangelism and social justice. Here I renewed my call to ministry.

Two great blessings came during my six-year pastorate in Hancock County. First, I progressed from serving as a "to be supplied" (week-to-week) pastor to licensed local pastor, and ordination as deacon and finally full elder. As though serving two churches each Sunday was not enough, I could not ignore Diamondhead, the fastest growing community on the Mississippi Gulf Coast, located equidistant from the two churches. We began holding early Sunday morning services and home Bible studies which led to the founding of Diamondhead United Methodist Church. This was the first of two UMC churches I had the honor of helping launch.

San Diego: Go West (not-so-young man)
In 1998, my wife Anita, a career-long civil servant with the Department of Defense, transferred to San Diego. I followed. After presenting myself to the San Diego District Superintendent, she informed me there were no pulpits open. Anita and I attended First United Methodist of San Diego for six months. It was a most spiritually uplifting time for me, and offered a much needed opportunity to participate in worship from the other side of the pulpit with my family.

In April 1999, the District Superintendent unexpectedly called, inquiring if I was still available and interested in serving a church. Of course I was, even though I had a full-time job as technology manager and taught graduate courses at San Diego State. The Bishop appointed me to Christ United Methodist Church of San Diego, effective July 1, 1999.

From Christ Church to Christ Ministry Center

As with many urban churches, times had changed at Christ Church from the 1960s, the high point of church participation in America. Once a thriving church, home to 700 members, Christ Church had more funerals than baptisms, more people moving out of the neighborhood, and less money in the offering plate, year after year. It was not for lack of effort or leadership, but the unavoidable result of urban changes in an increasingly secular society.

Here was a large church building in the heart of San Diego that was used basically for one hour on a Sunday morning. Some rooms in the education building had not been used in decades.

By 2005 it was inevitable that Christ Church in San Diego would eventually close. But God impressed upon me our dwindling congregation should take a radically different path. It would require great faith and operating in uncharted waters.

In response to an article by The Rev. Shane Stanford, I realized there was no time left to wait. Shane's article was the catalyst to share a new vision with the congregation. In his "wake up call", Shane identified five survival issues congregations would face over the next 10 years. Keep in mind that was in 2005, well before the great recession of 2008, and in hindsight, proved Shane was prophetic. Those issues included:

- The "Graying of the Church"
- Personal Financial Dysfunction
- Technology Impact
- Capital Investment for Facility Improvements and Maintenance
- Stewardship Resource Development

On May 23, 2005, I shared my emerging vision with the congregation in the weekly e-newsletter. I proposed to our members *"a new model for us as Christ UMC 'Ministry Center', where four congregations, a half dozen weekday ministries for youth, women, refugees, and the economically oppressed, plus twelve step organizations who help people win victories over addictive behavior, unite to do far more together than any of us can do alone...to the honor and glory of our Lord Jesus Christ."*

Christ Ministry Center was born.

A decade later, Christ Ministry Center is officially a reality. We hold a charter from the United Methodist church, are a legal corporation in the

State of California, and have our own 501(c)(3) non-profit designation with the Internal Revenue Service.

Now we are home to not four, but a dozen multi-ethnic congregations of various faiths, and provide office space and conference rooms to another dozen charities. Combined, we serve over 1,200 people a week.

SECTION ONE: Ministry Center Basics

Chapter 1: What Is a Ministry Center?
(Defining Ministry)

"Then shall the King say unto them on his right hand, Come, ye blessed of my Father, inherit the kingdom prepared for you from the foundation of the world: For I was hungry, and ye gave me meat: I was thirsty, and ye gave me drink: I was a stranger, and ye took me in: Naked, and ye clothed me: I was sick, and ye visited me: I was in prison, and ye came unto me. Then shall the righteous answer him, saying, Lord, when saw we thee hungry, and fed thee? or thirsty, and gave thee drink? When saw we thee a stranger, and took thee in? or naked, and clothed thee? Or when saw we thee sick, or in prison, and came unto thee? And the King shall answer and say unto them, Verily I say unto you, in as much as ye have done it unto one of the least of these my brethren, ye have done it unto me." (Matthew 25:34-40, King James Version)

The first question members asked when I proposed Christ Church become a "Ministry Center" in 2005 was, *"What is a Ministry Center?"* I was not completely sure. But I had faith God placed us in the heart of San Diego to do something different than keep on doing what we had been doing; waiting until the last member died, close the doors, turn off the lights, and sell the building.

Those faithful folks deserved a more definitive "From Church to Ministry Center Plan" than I could offer then. They placed their trust in God that the Holy Spirit was guiding us upon our own exodus; a journey through uncharted wilderness to an unseen promised land.

Convincing the congregation to take this leap of faith was only the first step. As Methodists, the Conference says when a church is born and when it closes because the denomination owns the building. So when I shared the emerging Ministry Center vision with my District Superintendent and Bishop, they too asked, *"What is a Ministry Center?"*

Once again, the response was, *"I'm not completely sure, but if we trust God's leadership in this, we will find out together."* Without the support of my District Superintendent and Bishop and their successors, Christ Ministry Center would never have happened.

Something Old

"Ministry Center" is a new way of realizing an old, abiding and perpetual truth. The mission of the church Jesus proclaimed 2,000 years ago still works!

"Go therefore and make disciples of all nations, baptizing them in the name of the Father and of the Son and of the Holy Spirit, teaching them to observe all that I have commanded you; and lo, I am with you always, to the close of the age." (Matthew 28:19-20 RSV)

The Kingdom of God is among us. I proposed we rediscover vitality through loving God and loving our neighbors. The plan we would follow is simple, but not easy: feeding the hungry, quenching spiritual thirst, clothing the naked, caring for the sick, visiting the imprisoned and welcoming strangers who just might be angels in disguise (Matthew 25:35 and following). Miracles happen when we touch lepers and forgive the fallen. Then, and only then, will the world respond to our preaching and teaching. That is when churches, seeking to save their lives, find new life by losing it…for Christ's sake. Pope Francis reminds us by his example the world still responds to genuine love and discipleship.

Something New

Like too many congregations, Christ Church was in the fast lane to being closed, the building sold, and money spent to cover increasing denominational debts. As almost always happens, a new congregation – likely ethnic and more evangelical if not Pentecostal – would buy the building and fill the sanctuary within a few months.

Why couldn't we do with our church what someone else would do in short order after we close?

That is the fundamental question facing churches today. And the answer must be based upon what God wants for your church more so than just what you want.

In documenting the Christ Ministry Center model, my goal is that it may offer both hope and a way forward for hundreds of churches that will otherwise "go out of business" over the next decade.

For the last half-century, Mainline Protestants have been a lot better at closing churches than revitalizing existing ones or starting new ones. Two of my friends are realtors who specialize in selling closed church buildings.

One recently shared that there are 96 churches for sale in Southern California. How long they sit on the market is rapidly decreasing, indicating the demand for a constant supply of vacant houses of worship.

When churches close, we cede hard won ground gained by the toil, sweat, tears and sacrifice of generations before us.

This is not to imply churches are not working to survive and thrive. Too many, however, are using tactics from the 1950s to 1970s that simply do not work any longer. Between the time I became pastor of Christ Church in 1999 and 2005 when we adopted the Ministry Center plan, we tried many ways to reverse the decreasing membership. Too many churches have their eyes in the rear view mirror, one of several danger signs I identify in the Ministry Center model.

God did not call me to Christ Church to preside over her funeral; at least not without a fight. Knowing what battles to fight is critical. The seven last words of a dead church are always, *"We Never Did It That Way Before."* Yet too many churches prove insanity because they keep doing the same thing over and over, hoping for a different result.

Characteristics of a Ministry Center
A decade after being asked *"What is a Ministry Center?"* I am better prepared to answer that question.

Here are some characteristics of a Ministry Center.
- A Ministry Center is a church that changes its primary focus from the building and Sunday morning to seven-days-a-week discipleship and service.
- A Ministry Center is a church that recognizes it is God's church more than "my church", and boldly trusts God's leadership.
- A Ministry Center becomes a place where the community finds food for both their bodies and souls rather than just a place to 'hold church services'.
- A Ministry Center surrenders control so that it may become a dynamic entity open to the workings of the Holy Spirit and daily divine intervention.
- A Ministry Center forms alliances with other churches, charities and social agencies to be better stewards of time, energy and resources.

- A Ministry Center is a church where diversity, as at Pentecost, empowers people from all walks of life to find a spiritual home in their community.
- A Ministry Center is open to non-traditional opportunities and is willing to "think outside the box".
- A Ministry Center redirects its energy from survival and maintenance to thriving and abundance.

There are more characteristics, methods and rewards to becoming a Ministry Center.

On The Outside Looking In
It was on a weekday afternoon in 2002. I passed through the "welcome room" at the rear of our sanctuary. I saw a girl, about eight years old, a member of our after-school program, peeking into our sanctuary. *"Hi,"* I said. My voice startled the little girl, having been transfixed by trying to take in all that she saw in our worship center, decorated for Easter services. She apologized for staring into the inner sanctum of our church. In words that broke my heart, she said, *"Pastor Bill, do you think one day I could actually go into the church? You see, my family doesn't go to church, and I've never been inside."* Fighting back tears, I said, *"Sweetheart, you sure can. Let's do it now."* She delighted in her personal guided tour, thanked me, and ran outside telling her playmates the excitement she could not contain. I remember her often, and wonder if that remains her solitary venture into God's Holiness.

I often wonder how many of our neighbors are on the outside, looking into our churches. But for whatever reason, they do not feel comfortable or worthy to come inside.

I also hope I never lose her excitement of being in God's house, something we too easily take for granted.

Chapter 2: What Are Our Options?
(Exploring Choices)

"Trust GOD from the bottom of your heart; don't try to figure out everything on your own. Listen for GOD's voice in everything you do, everywhere you go; he's the one who will keep you on track. Don't assume that you know it all. Run to GOD! Run from evil! Your body will glow with health; your very bones will vibrate with life! Honor GOD with everything you own; give him the first and the best. Your barns will burst; your wine vats will brim over." (Proverbs 3:5-10)

All churches, and especially struggling ones, have three options. First, keep on doing what you have been doing. Second, face reality and make the difficult choices which may include closure. Third, re-think church and step out on faith to find new purpose and vitality.

The Four Lepers
In 2 Kings 7, four lepers were caught between the besieged city of Samaria and the Syrian army. The citizens had thrown the lepers outside the city wall. There they were caught between three apparently bad options. If they went back into the city, they would be killed. If they just sat there, they would die. And if they threw themselves upon the mercy of the Syrians, they may die, but maybe they would find pity. Struggling churches see themselves as caught between poor options. But God often has surprises when people act upon their faith.

"It happened that four lepers were sitting just outside the city gate. They said to one another, "What are we doing sitting here at death's door? If we enter the famine-struck city, we'll die; if we stay here we'll die. So let's take our chances in the camp of Aram and throw ourselves on their mercy. If they receive us we'll live, if they kill us we'll die. We've got nothing to lose."

So after the sun went down they got up and went to the camp of Aram. When they got to the edge of the camp, surprise! Not a man in the camp! The Master had made the army of Aram hear the sound of horses and a mighty army on the march. They told one another, "The king of Israel hired the kings of the Hittites and the kings of Egypt to attack us!" Panicked, they ran for their lives through the darkness, abandoning tents, horses, donkeys—the whole camp just as it was—running for dear life. These four lepers entered the camp and went into a tent. First they ate and drank. Then they grabbed silver, gold, and clothing, and went off and hid it. They came back, entered another tent, and looted it, again hiding their plunder.

Finally, they said to one another, "We shouldn't be doing this! This is a day of good news and we're making it into a private party! If we wait around until morning, we'll get caught and punished. Come on! Let's go tell the news to the king's palace!" (2 Kings 7:3-9)

For struggling churches, going back seems like a good choice. The past is known and offers the comfort of familiarity. But no matter how hard you try to go back, it simply doesn't work. And most likely it assures you will perish.

Just sitting still is not a good option ether. Waiting for fate to overtake you only means it is just a matter of time until the end comes.

The third option, boldly steeping out on faith, is frightening, but offers the best prospect of finding the abundant blessings of God.

Discerning God's Will for Your Church
Discerning God's will for the future of your church is the most critical part of this process. It is not just your decision or that of your congregation alone. The will of God should be determined. Then everything else will fall into place.

Of course, if you determine it is not God's will that you become a Ministry Center, then don't do it! If you discern that staying the current course will lead to the inevitable closure of your church, then you make the best use of your remaining time until the end or explore other options. There are no easy decisions, for whatever you decide, there will be struggles, sacrifice and possibly grief.

How do you determine God's will for your church? The best place to start is on your knees in prayer.

Apart from spiritual discernment, we offer some assessments that will help you take an objective look at your current situation and prospects for future success as a Ministry Center.

Churches have lifecycles. They are conceived, born, grow, prosper, plateau, decline, and may eventually die. Even churches that have been around a long time have gone through death-rebirth-and-resurrection experiences as customs, culture, technology and neighborhoods change.

The church that my ancestors helped build and attended recently celebrated their 175th Anniversary. My great-grandfather would not recognize that church today. Not only has the building gone through remodeling and upgrades, the worship is unlike anything he knew. Even if they sing the old hymns, churches now use electric keyboards, loudspeakers and overhead projection that would scare the dickens out of Great-Grandpa Jenkins.

Option One: "To live is Christ..." (Philippians 1:21a)
The first option is to hold on and hope for a better day.

In the Parable of the Talents (Matthew 25) Jesus told the story of a master who gave three servants "talents" (equal to a thousand dollars each). To one he gave five talents, to another servant, two talents, and yet another servant one talent. When he returned from his journey, this master called for an accounting of his investments. The servant who received five talents wisely invested and returned the original five talents, plus five more. Likewise, the servant who received two talents was a good steward and produced the original two talents, plus two more. But the servant who received one talent was so cautious he might fail, he dug a hole and buried the talent. The master was angry.

"The master was furious. 'that's a terrible way to live! It's criminal to live cautiously like that! If you knew I was after the best, why did you do less than the least? The least you could have done would have been to invest the sum with the bankers, where at least I would have gotten a little interest. 'take the thousand and give it to the one who risked the most. And get rid of this "play-it-safe" who won't go out on a limb. Throw him out into utter darkness." (Matthew 25:26-29, The Message).

Churches whose strategy is just to "hold on" will always fail. Sure, it's a risky world out there. But God expects his servants to have a bold vision and faith in the Lord's blessings. This requires faith that God will "provide the increase".

I told the folks at Christ Church San Diego that if they simply wanted to find a way to keep the doors open and the lights on, then they had the wrong minister. Too many dead and dying urban churches have found "revenue streams" that enable their ever dwindling congregation to "hold on" for a few more years. Trouble is, the church is still dead and dying, barely surviving on artificial life support systems.

Option Two: "…to die is gain." (Philippians 1:21b)
The second option is to graciously "let go".

Sometimes churches die. Some embrace the fact it is time to pull the plug on a church that is merely surviving on life-support. As difficult as it may be to reach that conclusion, Christians teach there is no need to fear death. *"O death, where is thy sting? O grave, where is thy victory?"* That holds true for Christians and churches.

Mark Sandlin, Presbyterian minister from Greensboro NC, wrote in a beautiful article for Sojourners entitled "To the dying church".

"Watching someone you love, who helped raise you, who cared for you when you weren't well, who partially defined who you would be, slowly perish before your eyes is difficult to say the least. I love you. I don't want to lose you.

"But, this is life. These things happen. Those you love do die. It's just how it works. I mean, there were churches before you. They may not have looked like you or sung songs like you or taught exactly what you do, but they all had Love – just different ways of expressing it. They changed people's lives. They made some people better people and, sometimes, they made people worse people. Then, they died.

"Death sucks. I'm going to miss you – so much – but I refuse to mourn you. You will always be with me. The Love that has always sought to be known is still with us. The spirit that is the church will go on – thrive, even. It will just look different and sing differently and teach differently, but it will go on. I really will miss you, truly, but I must admit I cannot wait to see what you will become on the other side. I'm so excited just thinking about the folks who will find new life in your new life. I get just a bit giddy thinking about the new places and space that Love will be shared. I get overwhelmed with joyfulness just thinking about the new ways you will learn to share Love.

"Maybe this kind of death is a blessing after all. It's so belovedly human to hold on so tightly to what we know that we constantly miss the opportunity to catch hold of something that might lead us to wider fields. How very God-like of God to make death the beginning of a blessing. So, just know, I

am here. We are here. You can let go. We will water the seeds. We will nurture the fields and then we can dance in them again, together."

Sometimes, it is necessary for an old church to die so new life can spring up. Christ Church voted to close so Christ Ministry Center could be born. That was a most gracious way to die. And, as you will read later, not only did the Ministry Center emerge, but a brand new dynamic and diverse United Methodist congregation arose from Christ Church's demise.

Option Three: "Thrive, not just survive"
The third option is when you discern that God wants your church to rethink your ministry. That's when you resolve to "thrive, not just survive". In the pages of this book, you will find resources and lessons learned that will inspire and empower your church to not just exist, but flourish.

If your church is committed to become a Ministry Center, God will surely prepare (anoint) you to succeed.

If your choice is to help your church thrive, not just survive, then the remainder of this book is dedicated to helping lead your church upon this awesome adventure of faith.

Lines of Expectations and Circles of Complacency
I once preached a sermon I entitled, "When God Gets Out of Line". God often acts outside the lines of our expectations, defying our limited faith and myopic vision. As difficult as it is to admit, in that regard, we are just like the Pharisees who constantly challenged Jesus about who, what, where, when and how he could perform miracles. The end result is we either do not recognize, or do not accept, the miracles God performs in our daily lives.

When we sit in our circles, whether in Bible study or committee meetings (necessary and worthy events in church life), we must look beyond the circle to the world Jesus loved and offered his life. I am amazed at how passionate churches become about which side of the chancel the piano is on, the color of new paint in the fellowship hall, and about who does and does not have access to certain rooms in the church. That is a church sitting in a closed circle, focused on itself, its needs and its possessions. Many of those same churches fail to see the weeping young mother, the struggling older man at our door.

Sometimes Jesus acts "out of line" to disrupt our comfortable circles of complacency.

Climbing Jacob's Ladder
The story of Jacob's ladder provides an excellent framework to explore how God wants us to "climb up higher" in recovering vitality in the declining church.

Higher Dreams – Dreams played an important role in the Bible. Many times, God used dreams to show visions of where people were to go. A sad reality is that, as we get older, we forget how to dream, and become increasingly cynical. The Bible speaks of a time when *"your OLD MEN will dream (new) dreams"*. That's quite a feat: to have OLD men dreaming new dreams. I am now an old man, but I am still dreaming new dreams of what God can do. As a university professor, I found far too many of my students, many who were half my age, who have already given up on their dreams. Jacob's renewed dream was a turning point in his life. Struggling churches need to "Dream Higher".

Are you a dreamer or a cynic? Do you expect great things from God and attempt great things for God? Or do you say, *"Ain't no use trying. Nothing ever turns out right no-how."* Climb up higher.

Higher Commitment – Up until the "ladder dream", Jacob was immature, "playing games" with his brother, Esau, and his parents, Isaac and Rebecca. Now, because of his foolishness, Jacob was literally running for his life. (It's difficult to see the goal when you are running in survival mode.) After this encounter with God, Jacob "grew up" and accepted responsibility for his own spiritual life. He quit blaming others, and making excuses. He set about to mend broken relationships, make wrongs right, and (most importantly) complete God's will for his life. In short, he took responsibility for his life, his happiness, and his spiritual growth. Struggling churches need to climb up to a higher level of commitment.

Higher Awareness – When Jacob awoke from his dream, God reminded Jacob of His purpose for Jacob's life. Jacob erected an altar there, and named the place Beth-El (House of God). The saddest part of the whole story is when Jacob lamented, *"Surely God was in this place, and I DID NOT KNOW IT"*. We need a higher awareness that we walk with God, for He is before us, behind us, beneath us, and above us at all times.

Are you aware that God is IN YOUR PLACE? If not, climb up higher.

Our Prayer for Renewed Faith

Lord, if we are living in Ezekiel's valley of dried bones, focused on the dust of the unimportant, the relics of religion rather than the Spirit Who gives new life, please act out of line, breathing new life into my parched and weary soul so that I may see your mission beyond the comfort of my complacency. Give me a new set of expectations of what you can, rather than what you cannot do. Help us "muster" a mustard seed of faith. Help us erase the lines we have drawn to segregate those things that are "mine" from those that should be everyone's. O Lord, all I am and all I have are yours. Use me and my meager possessions as instruments of your amazing love and grace to all mankind. Amen.

Chapter 3: What If We Rethink Church?
(Rethinking Church and Ministry)

What if church was less about Sunday, and more about the other days of
the week?

What if church wasn't just a place we go, but something we do.
A menu of adventure.
An active verb, instead of a noun.

What if Church wasn't just a building, but thousands of doors, each
opening to a different concept or experience of church, so that whoever
knocks might find a journey to call their own.

What if church was the way church was in the beginning?
Outbound, Unbound, Active.
Human beings from completely different worlds, united by common
purpose, experience and belief. Creating real solutions for their daily lives.

What if church looked at itself with seekers' eyes?
Recognizing that even the smallest step through one of our doors is an act
of courage, a moment of vulnerability.

That solving a secular need can lead to spiritual interaction.
That social relationships can offer opportunities for discussions of faith,
and provide inspiration for discovery.
And that for a skeptical world, actions often do speak louder than words.

What if church was more of an out-of-church experience?
An opportunity to prove what we say we believe, with our lives.

Then, perhaps, Sunday could be a day of rest and reflection on all that we
had accomplished Monday through Saturday.

What if we rethink church?
Not in terms of what it is, but what it could be.
And what if we can convince the world to do the same?

Together we can open hearts, open minds, and open doors.
The people of The United Methodist Church

SECTION TWO: Ministry Center Vision

Chapter 4: What Are the Universal Principles?
(Guiding Values)

"To make sure your foundation is trust in God; I'm laying it all out right now just for you. I'm giving you thirty sterling principles— tested guidelines to live by. Believe me—these are truths that work, and will keep you accountable to those who sent you." (Proverbs 22:19-21)

Based upon our decade long transformation from church to Ministry Center, we had to address many critical matters. Some had relatively minor consequences in the overall picture. However, we found that there were critical, essential matters confronting us.

Here is an overview of the "Seven Guiding Principles" that apply to most, if not all, who are considering the path from church to Ministry Center. We explore each of these in detail in Chapters 5 through 11.

Here is a preview of the issues you must consider if you plan to become a Ministry Center.

1. The "Ministry Center Model"
So why is having this or another model important? We found that having the Ministry Center Model helped form the foundation of Christ Ministry Center. It focused our efforts and organized our ministries.

Have as many ministries focused around hunger, thirst (including spiritual thirst), clothing, wellness, prison and befriending strangers as possible.

In Chapter 5, we look at the Ministry Center Model. It will look familiar, because it comes from Matthew 25. We have many ministries focused around hunger, thirst (including spiritual thirst), clothing, wellness, prison and befriending strangers.

But the most important things that occurred when we adopted the Ministry Center Model were the "God things" that began to happen. Rather than us seeking churches, charities and social agencies to join us, those organizations began coming to us. We saw the Holy Spirit at work, building upon Christ's model.

2. It is God's Church

We all form emotional attachments to our home church, but the building, traditions or rituals are never a substitute for genuine ministry.

In Chapter 6, we look at "whose church is this anyway?" Is it God's church? Is it my church? Is it the denomination's or local congregation's church? Answering that question will empower, or disqualify your church as a Ministry Center.

3. Relinquish Control

Declining churches do not have the resources to do everything they want or need to do. We discovered when we ceased trying to do everything ourselves and control everything and everybody under our roof that God provided the help. We needed to trust other groups to do what they do best without trying to control them.

At Christ Ministry Center, a grocery distribution ministry (I was hungry), a women's prison ministry (I was in prison), a clothes charity (I was naked), new churches (I was spiritually thirsty), a health screening service (I was sick) and ethnic congregations (I was a stranger) all suddenly appeared. They were experts in doing what they do far better than we could ever do it!

In Chapter 7 we show how declining urban churches need to trust other groups to do what they do best without trying to control them.

4. Thrive, Don't Just Survive

Keeping the doors open is not an indication of vital ministry. Many dying urban churches find ways to prolong their existence while avoiding facing the reality of failure to connect with their changing neighborhood and culture.

In Chapter 8, we illustrate seven areas of where the Ministry Center allows a struggling church to thrive, not just survive.

5. Get Down and Dirty

There is no sanitized way of doing urban ministry or any ministry, for that matter. Expect that often those in greatest need may appear the least lovable.

In Chapter 9, we show how the Ministry Center allows churches to reach the downtrodden and despised in ways the conventional church is not prepared to do. Following Jesus' example of touching lepers, befriending tax collectors and sinners, both the church and the community will become transformed.

6. Think Abundance, not Scarcity

Jesus took two loaves and five fish to feed five thousand (just counting the men). There is an abundance of help out there being provided by churches, charities and social agencies but it needs to be coordinated.

In Chapter 10, we show how to quit focusing on what you do not have and recognize the abundance God has provided right at your doorstep. Also, in Chapter 26, we offer an in-depth look at The Fount of Blessings. We offer a practical way for your church to become part of a nationwide network of churches, charities and social agencies helping the hungry, homeless, hurting and helpless through The Fount of Blessing (MyFount.com). "The Fount" began at Christ Ministry Center and now helps people locate food, clothing, shelter and many more essentials in all 50 states.

7. Trust God

Urban ministries will always struggle to survive, much like those we are called to help. Revenues will come and go. Charities and congregations will, too. Anxiety is the opposite of faith.

In Chapter 11, we will show you how to trust God as you make the challenging transition from church to Ministry Center.

Chapter 5: What is the Ministry Center Model?
(Modeling Ministry)

"Then the King will say, 'I'm telling the solemn truth: Whenever you did one of these things to someone overlooked or ignored, that was me—you did it to me.'" (Matthew 25:40)

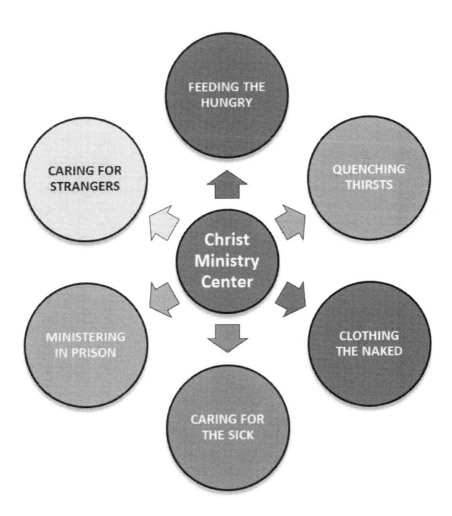

It helps to have a blueprint when building something new. For Christ Ministry Center, that blueprint emerged when we recognized a familiar pattern as God brought churches and charities into partnership with us.

As it turned out, the model is not new at all. It's been around for 2,000 years. Matthew 25 is the basis of the Ministry Center Model. I call it "life's final exam". The way Matthew records it, these are the questions Jesus asks at the "pearly gates" that determines who gets into heaven, and who does not.

"Then he will say to those on his left, 'Depart from me, you who are cursed, into the eternal fire prepared for the devil and his angels.

> *For I was hungry and you gave me nothing to eat,*
> *I was thirsty and you gave me nothing to drink,*
> *I was a stranger and you did not invite me in,*
> *I needed clothes and you did not clothe me,*
> *I was sick and in prison and you did not look after me.'*

"They also will answer, 'Lord, when did we see you hungry or thirsty or a stranger or needing clothes or sick or in prison, and did not help you?' He will reply, 'truly I tell you, whatever you did not do for one of the least of these, you did not do for me.' Then they will go away to eternal punishment, but the righteous to eternal life." (Matthew 25:40-46, New International Version)

This is the basis of the Ministry Center Model.

A Ministry Center is a seven-day-a-week 'church' that is engaged in one, all, or more of these ministries. Here is how this shapes out at Christ Ministry Center.

I was hungry…

Rather than trying to start our own food ministry with a small, aging congregation with limited resources, God sent Crossroads Christian Ministries to us. Their ministry is to collect near-expiration food from grocery stores and give it to those who would otherwise go hungry. Crossroads needed a distribution place where they could unload and distribute food. CMC is an ideal location, right in the heart of San Diego near four freeways with off street parking. Crossroads has its own volunteers who arrive on Tuesdays and Fridays, set up, distribute the groceries, and then clean up. Their Tuesday distribution is for other churches or charities who take van loads of food to either their congregations or to orphanages across the nearby border in Mexico. Their Friday distribution is for the general public. Anyone, whether they can pay a modest 50 cents to $2.00 donation to help cover gas, receives a "banana box" full of bread, vegetables, fruit, and other food. No questions asked. No ID required. And since Crossroads doesn't "count noses" we do not know how many people each week are blessed. Conservatively, 250 or more are less hungry as the result of this ministry. In addition, Exodus Church maintains a food pantry that is available weekdays and Sundays.

I was thirsty...

It took a while to see how this ministry fits the model. After all, if we give you a loaf of bread, of course we will give you a cup of water to "wash it down". God revealed this part of the model is not about H2O. It is quenching "spiritual thirst" in the same way as with the woman at the well in John 4. This is where the dozen congregations and ministers fit into the model. Through their worship, fellowship, Christian education, counseling, evangelism and outreach, hundreds of lives are touched each week. At least 500 people attend worship each week with one of these churches. Since CMC is an incubator for homeless churches, we rejoice when a church outgrows our facilities and moves on to a larger home.

I was naked...

Many churches have clothes closets. CMC is no exception. Christ Chapel, the legacy congregation of Christ Church, continues to operate 'My Brother's Keeper' clothes closet where people walk in off the street and find clothes for the whole family. In addition, Dress for Success of San Diego is a strategic partner. Dress for Success serves women through career coaching, life skills training, and providing appropriate dresses or suits for job interviews. CMC provides a large wardrobe room and dressing room. In turn, CMC refers ladies to Dress for Success who may then access their wardrobe and career services. Crossroads also distributes clothing. It's another win-win.

I was sick...

CMC formed a strategic alliance with a neighborhood health clinic and with LifeLine Screening. During open enrollment, CMC becomes a satellite campus for the neighborhood clinic to enroll the uninsured in medical insurance programs. At the same time, they provide basic health screening for such things as high blood pressure. LifeLine Screening uses CMC's Social Hall quarterly for a day long health screening. Using their proprietary procedures, LifeLine serves about 60 people per visit. They often detect life threatening health issues, such as blocked arteries. In addition to these health ministries, CMC offers a prayer and healing ministry called Balm of Gilead.

I was in prison...

One of the most amazing alliances formed at CMC is with Welcome Home Ministries. Welcome Home is a women's prison ministry formed in 1990. While recidivism at San Diego's Las Colinas women's jail is 90%, recidivism among the women in Welcome Home's FAIR dorm is 10%. It is when a woman is released from jail that she is most vulnerable, particularly without a support system. Often family and friends abandoned the women when they were arrested, especially if they serve an extended sentence. Upon reentry, many have no choice but to return to the habits and environment that got them in trouble originally. In a bold alliance, Welcome Home and CMC have become the "first stop, one-stop" for women re-entering the community. Welcome Home will meet the women at the county jail gate upon their release. If they do not have food, clothing, shelter or spiritual support, the ladies come to CMC where they find resources to make a new start in life. We become their support system until they get their feet firmly settled in a new and better life.

There are many people trapped in prisons of their own making. While they are not behind metal bars, they are incarcerated by addictions and other man-made prisons. CMC is home to both Alcoholics Anonymous (AA) and Narcotics Anonymous (NA) groups. The NA group meets daily at 9:00 a.m. with an average attendance of 40. The AA group meets weekly with another 40 individuals participating. CMC is also the West Coast headquarters for Gambling Recovery Ministry, an Indiana based ministry that addresses one of the fastest growing and most devastating of all addictions. CMC provides a resource library for those impacted by gambling addiction.

I was a stranger...

One of the greatest impediments to church growth and survival is churches seek to find new members "of like kind". For instance, if a church has been made up of white, middle class, well-educated tithers, and keeps holding out for finding new members who are the same, it will find the odds are stacked against them. That is especially true in the urban environment. Too many churches die because they do not welcome strangers! That is another way of saying churches most often close when they do not welcome and assimilate the changing demographics of their neighborhood.

We learned a great lesson when a large group of Haitians came to us seeking asylum. They were a Christian music group on tour, and were being persecuted in Haiti for trying to keep youths out of gangs, drug culture and human trafficking. By "welcoming strangers" we doubled our meager Sunday morning attendance! And oh, how the Haitians enriched and enlivened our worship with their music and enthusiastic participation. In welcoming the Haitians, a predominantly African-American congregation and a Hispanic congregation, a whole new, vibrant church emerged. The combined attendance in these four congregations grew to 200 weekly, replacing Christ Church's dwindling attendance. It is the closest thing to Pentecost I have experienced in my ministry, where Christian love transcends racial, language and cultural differences. You may read more of that story in Chapter 28.

"Compassion"
It was in March 2009 I met a small group of Haitians at Christ Church who were seeking a church home in San Diego. From that first encounter, we established a bond that reached a climax January 10, 2010, as we rushed to the church for early reports of the devastating earthquake in their homeland, Haiti.

Over that next week, we practically lived at the church, praying, singing, and hoping as we impatiently watched for news of loved ones in Haiti. That includes three members of our Haitian ministry who had the misfortune of scheduling a trip to Haiti that placed them in the middle of the disaster. We rejoiced to learn they were all OK.

Although our Haitian Mission has about 60 active members, Christ Church has become the hub of the Haitian community in San Diego, which includes about 2,000 people.

When we opened our doors, hearts and minds to our Haitian brothers and sisters, they not only became members of our church, they became family. We worked closely with Immigration and Customs Enforcement (ICE) and the Immigration Courts to make sure these refugees and asylees observed immigration laws and had their day in court. We provided housing, food, clothes, training and health care. It was costly in both time and money. But it was one of the most rewarding investments we have ever made. It is still paying dividends as the Haitian Methodist Ministry of San Diego, a part of Exodus UMC and Christ Ministry Center, continues to bless and enrich our worship and service.

I am proud that America takes the lead in helping our brothers and sisters in Haiti and anywhere on the globe whenever disaster strikes. I'm proud to be United Methodist, because we are almost always the first to arrive and the last to leave when disasters strike.

Today we have Ethiopian, Eritrean, Marshallese, Hispanic, Haitian, African-Americans and Anglos sharing a common home. We have been home to Methodists, Baptists, Catholics, Anglicans, Pentecostals, Independent and Orthodox congregations.

And Much More...

In addition to this model, we are blessed to have other ministries whose focus is on helping abused women, vulnerable children, economic and environmental justice, and remarkably an alternative high school for at-risk children, operated jointly by the County Office of Education and Juvenile Court that meets in our building with 100 students and faculty on weekdays year round.

Trusting the Holy Spirit

Notice we have at least one church or charity whose primary focus is upon hunger, spiritual thirst, clothing the naked, caring for the sick, visiting those in prison, and welcoming strangers. That is not by accident. Once we submitted ourselves to God's will and plan, the Holy Spirit brought just the right people into partnership with CMC so God could bless hundreds of people each week.

Please notice I have not used the words "run" or "control" in reference to these ministry partners. We have no desire to "control" them. They do what they do far better than we could ever do. The "control" factor is one of the greatest hindrances to church survival. If you insist on controlling everything under your roof, you limit your potential to your time, energy and financial resources. But if you are willing to "lose your life, for Christ's sake" you most like will discover in so doing, as we did, a far better life than ever imagined.

Finally, you may discover another model. But we found having a model brings cohesion to everything we do. You are invited to adapt our model or create your own. Just be sure you adapt it to your unique situation.

Chapter 6: Whose Church is This, Anyway?
(Recognizing "God's Church")

"I see what you've done. Now see what I've done. I've opened a door before you that no one can slam shut." (Revelations 3:8)

There is an old saying, *"The way you see the problem IS the problem!"* The way your congregation sees themselves can be a blessing and a curse. A critical step in transformation from church to Ministry Center is to have a clear understanding of whose church your church is.

Is It MY Church, The Denomination's Church, or God's Church?

It makes a huge difference if you see your church as (1) "MY church", (2) the denomination's church or (3) God's church. In reality, it can be all three at the same time. But it is not so much what you and your church members say, but how you say it (and how you "live" it) that makes the critical difference. One response is an indication of personal ties and emotions. Another response addresses the legal status of church property. And the final response deals with the spiritual dynamics of a local church.

It's "MY" Church

The first response indicates the emotional ties and memories we have attached to our church.

What could possibly be wrong with identifying the church as "MY" church? I often hear faithful members say, *"I grew up here. I poured in my time, offerings, attendance, support and Christian service into this church for decades. And so did my family. My parents' funerals were conducted here. I was married here. My children were baptized here."* This first response, "It's MY church", is filled with emotional ties and memories.

It is a good and normal thing when members love their church. However, there are two potential dangers.

First, the personal pronoun "my" may indicate it is "more mine" than anyone else. And that often leads to excluding others who could bless your church by making it theirs, too. Many churches, without being aware and without intentionally doing so, set up an "us-them" dichotomy. The inability to attract, accept and assimilate "them" into "our" church is one of the major reasons churches decline and eventually close.

We have all seen toddlers playing with toys. One picks up a toy and another quickly grabs it and shouts "Mine!" It is human nature to hold on to what we believe is ours. But the parent sees this as an opportunity to teach the children to share.

The Ministry Center succeeds when its doors are wide open to all whom God sends your way. The Ministry Center helps turn "MY" church into "OUR" church, which includes "It's YOUR church, too."

Second, (and this is a bit harsh), the church building can overshadow the reason it exists. In Jesus' days, the temple had become more an object of worship than God. If the building is more important to us than the God we worship and serve, then it is idolatry!

In the next chapter, we look at how surrendering control is the pathway to success. That includes the church building.

One of the first battles faced when deciding to become a Ministry Center is coming to terms with rethinking "MY church". When I arrived at Christ Church, there were old Sunday school classrooms that no one had used for years. When I suggested we use those rooms as offices for charities or classrooms for other congregations, there was resistance in letting "them" use "our" rooms. Granted, no one was using the rooms. But some old timers held strong attachment to those spaces, remembering when the rooms were full on Sunday mornings many years ago. Working through such strong attachments will make the difference between those spaces remaining empty, locked in time, or seeing new life and new ministry.

The first response gets to the heart of ownership vs. stewardship. When a church sees itself as stewards of God rather than owners of a building, a Ministry Center can emerge.

It's the Denomination's or Congregation's Church
The second response deals with the legal ownership of the church property.

There are two basic forms of church governance: episcopal and congregational. In the episcopal churches (Catholic, Episcopal, Methodist, Lutheran, etc.), there is a "chain of command". Discerning the future of your church will have to include the approval and blessings of the hierarchy. In the congregational churches (Baptist, Congregational, Church of Christ, etc.), the local church owns the property and makes its own decisions regarding starting and closing churches. Each environment offers challenges and opportunities.

A Ministry Center may be born in either congregational or episcopal settings. Christ Ministry Center is owned by The United Methodist Church. Transition from Christ Church to Christ Ministry Center required denominational approval. As with all United Methodist churches and agencies, the church property is held in trust by the local trustees. Congregational churches, where the local church is the legal owner of the property, may independently decide to become a Ministry Center.

One of my District Superintendents years ago stated, *"We Methodists are resource rich and people poor!"* That sizes up the plight of many mainline denominations. We have large, beautiful churches that are virtually empty. Each year, we close and sell more church properties than start new ones.

The denomination cannot operate every struggling local church. Neither local churches nor Ministry Centers run themselves. Both require leaders, "boots on the ground" who are committed to being disciples in word and deed. Chapter 19 looks at what leadership is needed to operate a Ministry Center.

So while either the denomination or local church may own title to the church property, someone has to fulfill the steward's role in managing its operations.

It's God's Church
The third response gets to the spiritual and theological reason for the church's existence.

The scope of the local church's ministry increases when we see it as part of the Kingdom of God. The focus is less about temporal matters and more about fulfilling the mission of the church.

That's when we not only open our doors, but our hearts to the neighborhood and world. That's when barriers are broken down, lives are changed, wounds healed, and both bodies and souls are nourished.

Dave Ramsey, the nationally known Christian financial counselor, illustrates how "stewardship" came from King James era England, and has lost some of its original meaning. Ramsey says a "steward" was a supervisor hired by a medieval lord to manage his operations over a section of land. The lord owned the land; the steward managed the land for the lord.

The early King James Bible readers understood that imagery clearly. The Lord "owns" the church and has entrusted the management and care of his church to us.

It is easy to forget who really owns the church. When we begin believing and behaving as if we own the church, we fail. But when we "manage as ministry" the Lord's church, we succeed.

That's how a Ministry Center transforms a church's mission and future.

The "Real Church"

Our neighbors began to notice the changes as we became a Ministry Center. The changes were unfamiliar, and for some of them as with some of us, change is scary. One neighbor came into my office and said, *"I remember when this was a 'real church'."* I knew exactly what she meant. She had lived near the church for decades, and recalled when the neighbors got up on Sunday morning and filled the church for an hour. Those days are gone. I kindly asked her how long it had been since she or her neighbors had come to support that 'real church'. She smiled and admitted it had been decades. I replied to her, "You know, we are reaching far more people every week than the 'real church' ever reached, even in its hey-day. Not at 11:00 a.m. on Sunday, but many hours every day. Maybe, after all, we are now the 'real church'"!

Chapter 7: How to "Surrender Control and Win"
(Relinquishing Control)

"I see right through your work. You have a reputation for vigor and zest, but you're dead, stone-dead. Up on your feet! Take a deep breath! Maybe there's life in you yet. But I wouldn't know it by looking at your busywork; nothing of God's work has been completed." (Revelations 3:1-2)

In this chapter, the "surrender control and win" principle shows how we get far more accomplished through Ministry Center partnerships and alliances, which implies giving up control. And it is liberating, taking a huge burden off your shoulders.

Christ Church transformed to Christ Ministry Center, and it was simpler than anyone could have imagined. Simple, but it was not easy. Rather than holding on, we decided to let go. Rather than doing only what we could do and control ourselves, we decided to invite others, who do ministries better than anyone else, to minister here at the corner of Meade Avenue and 33rd Street in San Diego.

Controlling the church
Holding on is the ultimate act of control. And the longer you hold anything, be it money, or something tangible or intangible, the more difficult it is to let it go.

For legacy congregations, giving up control is most difficult. It looks too much like defeat and failure. They have been praying for a miracle. The answer to their prayers may not look anything like what they imagine. In fact, they may be telling God what the answer to their prayers is. Through the years, the distinction between the living God and church building has become blurred.

For the remaining few, often meeting God and the place where they meet God have become one and the same. It would be a sign of weak faith to change course after so long.

But the ultimate failure for a declining legacy congregation is "keeping on keeping on" until the last member is gone. That is the failure to save your church when there are ways to revitalize it.

"For whosoever will save his life shall lose it: but whosoever will lose his life for my sake, the same shall save it." (Luke 9:24) applies to churches as well as individuals.

Don't Be a "Control Freak"

"Control Freaks" are people who have an obsessive need to exercise control over people and circumstances, are often perfectionists, distrust others ability to perform as expected, micromanage, and have difficulty delegating. The urge to control is based in the fear of the unexpected. No one likes unpleasant surprises, so some try to control people and circumstances as a form of self-preservation. That almost always ends in disaster.

Control is a paradox. We think the more of life we control, the happier we will be. In fact, control brings with it more anxiety, unhappiness, and even anger.

Many of Jesus' teachings run contrary to the idea of control. Denying self, loving enemies, losing life in order to find it, poor vs. rich, first being last and last being first, and other teachings turn the desire to be in control on its head.

If you only conduct ministries that you can staff, fund and control, you greatly limit what your church will be able to do. If you give up controlling everything under your roof, trusting others to partner with you, you will transform your church into a Ministry Center. By giving up "control" we all get more done! It's a "win-win".

Flipping Churches

"Flipping houses" is one of the most popular genres of reality TV. HGTV has primetime episodes of "Fixer Upper", "Property Brothers", "Love It or List it", and "Flip or Flop" that show how old, dilapidated houses can be renovated or "flipped" to look like new, significantly increasing the market value of the house.

These programs focus on renovation – making an old, broken down house look new and re-purposed. I can't deny that what we have done at Christ Ministry Center has involved an enormous amount of new floors, plumbing, wiring, painting, and general repairs. But becoming a Ministry Center is much more than just cosmetic improvements and "curb appeal" for your church.

So perhaps a better illustration for what we hope to do in helping urban churches revitalize is "The Profit", a CNBC series where Marcus Lemonis (a savvy businessman) offers struggling small businesses capital investment and his expertise, often narrowly saving them from bankruptcy.

While Marcus often renovates the business storefronts, making the store (business) more efficient and pleasing to customers, his biggest contribution is in overhauling their manufacturing, marketing and business plan. Marcus' mantra is: "Business success is about the three P's: People, Process and Product." Of course, he also writes a fat check to clean up finances, for which he requires complete control to get things fixed and restore profitability.

But I am amazed at how many business owners who *seek* Marcus' advice *then do not take it.* Oh yes, they are willing to take his money, but often quickly fall back into the rut that had them on the brink of bankruptcy.

It's when the business owner is willing to "give up control" to someone with greater experience and expertise that the business begins to thrive. It is akin to "stepping out on faith".

But giving up control is so very difficult to do.

It reminds me of churches who continue their decline because their motto is, "We ain't never done it that way before!"

Chapter 8: How Do We "Thrive, Not Just Survive"?
(Thriving by Serving)

"I see what you've done, your hard, hard work, your refusal to quit. I know your persistence, your courage in my cause, that you never wear out. But you walked away from your first love—why? What's going on with you, anyway? Turn back! Recover your dear early love. No time to waste..." (Revelation 2:2-5)

Thriving in today's world is a notion beyond the range of possibilities for the average mainline church, especially those in urban settings. Most are in "survival mode" which precludes them from even considering becoming a vibrant congregation. Yet that is what God intended for every church at their birth. Somewhere along the way, too many have become lost.

Many struggling churches continue doing what they have been doing for decades. Change for them is too daunting. Other declining churches find ways to survive financially, and continue to operate mostly as usual. They continue to decline and delay their inevitable closure without discovering the keys to thriving.

The Ministry Center Model offers a dynamic third alternative: thriving.

Viability for a church is not always measured in attendees. Small congregation churches as well as mega-churches fulfill roles and purposes within God's Kingdom. The keys to thriving rest not so much in how many attend, but how well the church fulfills its mission. More important than its size, thriving vitality is a church's essential characteristic.

Based upon my experience, I share with you the following "Keys to Thriving, Not Just Surviving"

1. Thriving Demographics
The church began in Jerusalem at Pentecost. It began in the city as a multi-ethnic, multi-lingual church where the Holy Spirit transcended racial, linguistic, cultural and economic barriers. Today's church has mostly abandoned the city and is the most mono-ethnic organization in the community at 11:00 a.m. on Sunday.

As the world's population explodes, so does the decline and closure of churches. The modern church's greatest missed opportunity is failure to embrace migration. For centuries, the church sent missionaries to Africa,

Asia and South America to convert "the heathens". Today, the world has arrived at our doorstep. Raymond J. Bakke, the recognized authority on urban ministry, stated: *"Mission is no longer about crossing the oceans, jungles and deserts, but about crossing the streets of the world's cities. From now on, nearly all ministry will be cross-cultural amid the urban pluralism."*

It is easier said than done. But for the church that embraces diversity, the opportunities for thriving are abundant.

2. Thriving Opportunities

Ephesians 3:20-21 says, *"Now unto Him who is able to do exceeding abundantly beyond all that we ask or think, according to the power that works within us, to Him be the glory in the church and in Christ Jesus to all generations forever and ever. Amen."*

The traditional church has seen opportunities through narrow lenses often constrained by orthodoxy, prejudice and fear. Opportunities abound in every neighborhood. Sadly, many churches fail to see those opportunities. That can be deadly. For instance, a church located within the shadows of a major university closed. When I asked one longtime member why they did not become the campus church, she replied, *"We didn't want those HIPPIES coming into OUR church!"* The term "HIPPIE" shows how that church viewed its greatest potential constituency. They isolated themselves and doggedly chose to close rather than open their doors to hundreds of students who would have loved to make that church their home.

The persistent theme of abundance comes in play here. Far too many fail to see the abundance all around them. Like the disciples, they underestimated the potential of two fish and five loaves when 5,000 needed to eat.

3. Thriving Revenue

The traditional church passed the offering plate and had to live within the limits of those collections. Other churches found a hybrid method that combined offerings with other limited revenue streams, such as cell towers and shared rented worship space.

The Ministry Center Model offers a dynamic shift by offering a subtle, but significant, new revenue model. Chapter 12 goes into this new business model in greater detail. But stated briefly, operating revenues come from those who are in alliance with the Ministry Center, and not just from your members or from hybrid sources alone.

Christ Ministry Center has been self-supporting from its inception. It requires no additional denominational support, nor has it yet operated on funds from grants.

4. Thriving Methods

The traditional measures of church vitality have been worship attendance and offerings. The Ministry Center Model provides a new dynamic in measuring the extent of your church's mission.

Instead of seeing your church as 40 people sitting in a sanctuary designed for 400, you now realize you touch hundreds, if not thousands of lives each and every week. Sure, most of them may never sit in the pew on Sundays. But through the Ministry Center, scores are fed, clothed, and ministered unto.

And with technology and social media, you may reach far more each week through your website or social media. Streaming worship services over the internet is now affordable for the smallest of churches. One church that averages 110 in worship was delighted and surprised that the average "on line" participation in their worship was 143.

I stopped "counting noses" a long time ago. God alone knows the exact number of lives we touch each week. To God be the glory!

5. Thriving Connections

The traditional church has operated within the bounds of what it can accomplish by itself. Nothing has done more to erase the old boundaries of denominations as our common decline. Our theological differences are not as great as we once imagined when we accept, love and unite forces with other churches, charities and social agencies. Through genuine collaboration, the influence of a small congregation can be magnified a thousand fold.

This includes those churches and charities who become partners within the Ministry Center, and alliances with organizations whose focus is upon a shared ministry. For instance, Welcome Home Ministries focuses upon women's prison and re-entry ministry. They have an office in Christ Ministry Center. But both Welcome Home and CMC are members of the San Diego Reentry Roundtable, where we accomplish far more by joining efforts of the Sheriff's Department and 40 other agencies in San Diego whose mission is helping reentering former inmates.

6. Thriving Faith

We walk by faith, and not by sight. Faith is a virtue; something we do, not something we believe. When we surrender our lives to God's will, when we lose our lives for Christ sake, then and only then do we find our lives.

Becoming a Ministry Center can set your church free. Free from the tyranny of numbers. Free from the feeling of failure. Free from doom and despair. Free to live, both personally and collectively, as thriving, vibrant disciples of our Lord.

Jeremiah 29:11-13 says *"For I know the plans I have for you,"* declares the Lord, *"plans to prosper you and not to harm you, plans to give you hope and a future. Then you will call on me and come and pray to me, and I will listen to you. You will seek me and find me when you seek me with all your heart."*

7. Thriving Church Structure

The Ministry Center Model calls the church to step out of its comfort zone. It calls for creative thinking "outside the box". It calls for an entrepreneurial and ecumenical spirit. It means finding new ways to fulfill our timeless mission. Thriving means you are not being afraid to try something new. And even if it fails, we learn and grow.

We are called Methodists because we have a "method" for just about every potential circumstance that may arise within the church. There is one exception. We have no paragraph in the Book of Discipline on how to start and operate a Ministry Center.

Why do we have pages to tell us how to close churches and dispose of church property, but no paragraph to offer churches facing closure a way to "thrive, not just survive"? Journeying into uncharted waters is frightening. But the potential benefits are amazing. The journey through the wilderness is well worth finding the Promised Land.

"If we want to thrive; serve!"

I remember Annual Conference 2006 at Redlands, California. Bishop Mary Ann Swenson reminded us that *"If you wish to thrive, serve!"*

That is a time-tested Wesleyan principle. Many churches serve in densely populated areas. Yet we fail to thrive because we fail to serve. Most of our programs are geared to "come" when Jesus instructed us to "go". John

Wesley developed a massive following, not because of his well thought out theology, nor his finely tuned organization; but because he went about the "highways and byways" to widows, orphans, and dispossessed people of his day. His "street ministry" brought about vitality in ministry, just as Jesus' ministry did 2000 years ago.

As we look for ways to vitalize and re-vitalize our churches, the answer is not finding new formulas of preaching, music, or teaching. We don't need to appoint a new committee to discover why our committees are so ineffective. Tweaking the order of worship will not bring the masses through our doors and to our pews.

We don't need to schedule one more committee meeting to discuss scheduling another meeting on how to increase attendance. Bishop Swenson has the right idea: ""If you want to thrive; serve!"

Chapter 9: How Does a Ministry Center "Minister"
(Getting Down and Dirty)

"We pray that you'll live well for the Master, making him proud of you as you work hard in his orchard. As you learn more and more how God works, you will learn how to do your work. We pray that you'll have the strength to stick it out over the long haul—not the grim strength of gritting your teeth but the glory-strength God gives. It is strength that endures the unendurable and spills over into joy, thanking the Father who makes us strong enough to take part in everything bright and beautiful that he has for us." (Colossians 1:10-12)

Maggie Nancarro wrote in her blog the church is not so much dying as it is failing. There is a difference. Of course, any church that continues to fail will die and close. I believe there is as much "hunger and thirsting after God's righteousness" today as ever.

In what areas is the church failing? Sadly, the very place where seekers go to find an authentic encounter with God are often disappointed. It's not so much a matter of style of worship, denominational affiliation, or facilities. People still respond to "authentic" faith.

Maggie stated: *"Now we actually have to – authentically – feed people spiritually, emotionally, and physically to earn our keep in our society. Just like everyone else, we have to justify our existence. We can't expect to hold a position in society if we don't actually do what we say we're about."* (maggienancarro.com)

Christ Ministry Center can serve as a model for how dying inner-city churches may find renewal in ministry. But it has to be more than just keeping the doors open.

I can name urban churches that died years ago, but by extraordinary life support methods, similar to what is done in the ICU, they are being "kept alive" through artificial means. I know from first-hand experience ways inner-city churches can generate income to keep the doors open. But if the church is still dead, just keeping the doors open is not life. Not the kind of vibrant, empowering new life Jesus came to give to those who are spiritually dead.

Unless we are following Jesus' example of "getting down and dirty" in meeting the spiritual and physical needs of the poor and dispossessed, we are just going through the motions.

Jesus was not afraid to touch the lepers, cure the demon possessed, forgive the sinners, and care for women and children. He was familiar with the power of spittle's mud to restore sight to the blind. He got his hands dirty, while the religious leaders kept their pristine rituals from the comfort of the temple. He got his hands dirty to help the physical and spiritual needs of the dispossessed.

John Wesley brought about the most successful revival in church history by getting his hands dirty, caring for the street orphans and those in prison whom society had condemned and forgotten. Sure, he cared for their souls, too. But he did what the dead churches of his day had forgotten to do – care for both the body and soul.

Pope Francis has won the hearts of Catholics, Protestants and the world in general by touching and kissing the disfigured, the sick, and not shunning a little boy who wanted to share the stage with him during his homily.

It is dirty work, but someone has to do it.

How does a Ministry Center minister? How is it different from the manner a church usually ministers?

Strategic Partnerships and Alliances
Partners and Alliances play an important strategic role in the Ministry Center.

A Ministry Center stops trying to do everything by itself. The most amazing blessing we experienced was the discovery there are dozens of organizations in our community who wanted a place to conduct their programs. It was not by accident that God brought to us organizations whose mission was feeding the hungry, clothing the naked, quenching spiritual thirst, caring for the sick, the prisoner and the stranger. So we entered into partnerships with these wonderful organizations.

Partners
Partners are charities or organizations who conduct vital services, based upon our Ministry Center Model, and who pay little or no rent. They provide their own expertise, staff and volunteers.

Examples:

I was hungry:	Crossroads - grocery distribution charity
I was spiritually thirsty:	Churches - Worship, fellowship, counseling
I was naked:	Dress for Success - Clothes closet charity
I was sick:	LifeLine - health screening
I was in prison:	Welcome Home - Women's prison & re-entry
I was a stranger:	Alliance SD -Refugee service, ethnic churches

By becoming partners with these organizations, we immediately expanded the number of people reached, either directly or indirectly, each week. These partners do what they do better than we could do it. They are grateful to have a place to fulfill their mission. We are happy to enable them to do it. We step in when they ask, but we have no desire to "control" them. And we don't play the "Who gets credit?" game. We both agree, it's all about ministry, not about our egos.

There are other partners who call Christ Ministry Center home. Among these are a ministry focused upon battered women and at-risk children, an economic and environmental justice ministry, support groups, and an alternative high school where 100 students and staff attend on weekdays year round. Some of these are renters.

Alliances
In addition to the partners who "get down and dirty" daily, we are members of strategic alliances. These are coalitions of professionals, lawyers, social workers, advocates and faith leaders whose focus is upon meeting the same needs of our model in the greater community. By joining hands with these common purpose coalitions, the Ministry Center magnifies our impact within the community and world. Plus, our participation introduces us to community leaders we would otherwise never meet, makes us aware of available services, and informs us of issues at the city, county, state and national levels that may help or hinder our outreach to the poor.

Examples:

I was hungry:	San Diego Food Coalition
I was (spiritually) thirsty:	San Diego Region Interfaith Council
I was naked:	Clothes Recycling Service
I was sick:	Neighborhood Health Clinics
I was in prison:	San Diego Re-entry Roundtable
I was a stranger:	San Diego Immigrant Rights Consortium

From Cell to Celebration

Donna Cleveland's story would make a great book; and an even better movie. It is a classic account of how a person may rise from street-life to success.

A few years ago, not many would have expected Donna to be alive, much less receiving her Master's degree. They would not have been surprised to find her in jail, where she spent plenty of time. Only now, she has the keys to the same jail where she was incarcerated. And the keys to the hearts of dozens of women incarcerated in the Las Colinas Women's Jail in San Diego.

You might have guessed Donna is now a chaplain/social worker. The reason women in the Los Colinas listen to Donna is because she has been where they are, done most of the things they have done, and found a way out of "the street life".

As she sat in my office, I found it difficult to hold back tears listening to her testimony of how she cried out to God in the depths of despair. She thought she was beyond the love of God, and everyone else's love. That's when she met Carmen Warner-Robbins, founder and Director of "Welcome Home Ministries", an outreach specifically designed to help women in jail stay out of jail upon their release. But more than that, Welcome Home wants them to follow Donna's example in finding a better, abundant, successful life.

Donna acknowledges that through Carmen, she discovered the love of God, and now shares that love with dozens of women in prison. She is Carmen's associate in Welcome Home Ministries (based in Oceanside CA). Welcome Home has opened an office in Christ Ministry Center to serve their clients from the population center of San Diego County.

Donna is able to freely walk into and out of the jail that was literally her prison, now visiting inmates as no one else can do. She becomes the personification of hope for women with little hope. Donna, who once longed for and found the love of God, has a line of women now waiting for their hugs, their love, their living example of how life can change for the better.

Former San Diego County Sheriff Bill Kolender knew Carmen and Donna. He could not say enough good about their work. He reminded skeptics how much it costs to house one person for one year in jail. *"If Welcome Home* can help a fraction of these women, the financial benefits to taxpayers is significant," Sheriff Kolender said. But he knew, as did Carmen and Donna, it is not about the money. It is all about redeeming souls, so that many (trapped in drugs, abusive relationships and prostitution), may find the pathway Donna Cleveland has traveled, "From Cell to Celebration". That includes spiritual healing, without which most self-help strategies fail.

Through The Fount of Blessings
When we began to discover the abundant resources being offered by churches, charities and social agencies throughout the community, we wanted to share this vital information with both those in need and with the people helping them. In Chapter 27, you may learn more about The Fount of Blessings (MyFOUNT.com), a free website that enables anyone to find the abundant resources right in their neighborhood.

The good news is any church, charity, social agency or even an individual may use MyFOUNT.com and become a "Virtual Ministry Center" anywhere in the United States.

So how does a Ministry Center "minister"? It manages, but not by supervision and control. It manages through networking and synergy.
- Through the partner who has groceries, but no site to distribute them.
- Through a partner who wants to hold immigration rights forum, but has no venue or access to the people who need the information.

A Ministry Center (done right) has a vast network of people and organizations doing beneficial work. They put these people and organizations in touch with other groups (or provide physical spaces or publicity or some other helpful advantage) so that both the organization and the Ministry Center are blessed by the association.

Touching the Lepers
One Sunday, a man with AIDS showed up just before worship. It would have been easy to rush him along, because I needed to prepare for worship. Something within me said, "Take your time." We sat, and talked. I invited him to our service of healing.

At the end of the service, my new friend with AIDS and his wife came forward for anointing. After the service, as we parted, the man said what blessed him most was that I gave him a hug. "Pastor, you don't know how long it has been that anyone has touched me," he said. "Your embrace will do more to heal my body and soul than the anointing."

Messy Ministry

Mark Stowers wrote an article for the Jackson MS Clarion-Ledger in early June 2013 that asked if Jesus came to Jackson, where would he go? Mark suggested Jesus would show up at the Gateway Rescue Mission, the sort of place most "decent folk" try to avoid. It's an urban ministry where helping the helpless gets down and dirty, just like Jesus did on the streets of Jerusalem 2000 years ago.

Rex Baker began volunteering at Gateway 15 years ago. He fell in love with this "messy ministry", gave up a promising career in broadcast journalism, and now serves as executive director of Gateway's 27 employees and six centers covering three counties in metro Jackson.

Rex hit the nail on the head:
"Rescue mission life is real life played out in real time. We deal with broken people in all their messiness, and we reap the joy of seeing God work miracles. Gateway Rescue Mission is a place where fallen people minister a perfect Gospel to other fallen people."

"I like to think that if Jesus physically showed up in Jackson, Mississippi, He'd drop by Gateway Rescue Mission. Why? Because Jesus had this thing about hanging out with the wrong crowd. He associated with corrupt tax collectors, loose women, lepers...even Samaritans. He regularly shot off His mouth at the religious establishment. So yes, I think Jesus just might show up today at a crack house, have dinner with a leading drug dealer, or visit a rescue mission."

"If Jesus would do this, what should we do if we claim to be like Him? I'm far from perfect and fail daily in my feeble attempts to be like Christ. But I can read, and therefore know that Jesus says 'as much as you've done it unto the least of these brothers of Mine, you've done it unto Me.'"

"That's what we do at Gateway Rescue Mission. We feed hungry people, shelter the homeless, and work to restore the broken and addicted through the love of Christ. It's our calling as an organization. It's why we exist. We have staff who labor outside the spotlight because it's their calling in life."

So for anyone considering urban ministry, be forewarned: It takes some thick skin to do this kind of ministry. You will receive a lot more criticism than praise. And not everyone has your best intentions in mind. Just ask Mother Teresa or anyone else (like Rex) who deal with broken people in all their messiness and brokenness. The neighbors will not appreciate it; the critics will test your soul. Be prepared, and remember what God told Moses about the grumblers and gripers: *"Who are we in all this? You haven't been complaining to us—you've been complaining to God!"* *(Exodus 16:8)*

I would like to think if Jesus came to San Diego, he would hang out at Christ Ministry Center.

Chapter 10: How Do We "Think Abundance"
(Thinking Abundantly)

"I can see your pain and poverty—constant pain, dire poverty—but I also see your wealth. Fear nothing in the things you're about to suffer—but stay on guard! Fear nothing! Don't quit, even if it costs you your life. Stay there believing." (Revelation 2:9-11)

The greatest lesson I learned in all this was the lesson of abundance. It was to perceive the "unseen abundance" all around us. It was also to quit grousing about what we did not have and start seeing what Jesus promised, *"According to your faith, so be it unto you!" (Matthew 9:29).*

Too many churches and church leaders are pessimistic and focused upon what they do not have. *"We don't have enough people. We don't have enough money. We don't have enough energy."* Actually, the thing most lacking in many churches today is faith!

The principle of abundance permeates the Bible. Examples include:
- Promised land flowing with milk and honey
- Manna appearing daily
- The loaves and fishes
- The mustard seed of faith

Don't forget Jesus said, *"I have come that you might have life abundantly".* That abundance has little to do with money.

And the abundance is more than intangible. Physical blessings (food, clothes, etc.) abound. When we began connecting the dots that were forming the Ministry Center, we were amazed at how much abundance was out there being offered by churches, charities and social agencies. The problem usually was just the organization offering the food, clothes and so on knew when, where and how it was being offered.

Growing up in a family of nine in a four room shack in rural Mississippi, we learned some basic lessons about scarcity and abundance. We were poor. While many thought we had nothing of value, we had an abundance of almost everything; especially things money cannot buy: love, faith and hope for a better tomorrow. When David Roberts, my best buddy, came over to spend the night, Mother would just add some water to the soup and set another plate. And sleeping five boys in one room is not much more difficult than four. We had plenty to eat with chickens, hogs and vegetables all around. There were fish in the creek, wildlife in the woods, and wild berries and fruit ready for the picking.

My attitude toward abundance changed when I read, _Abundance: The Future is Better Than You Think_, by Peter Diamandis and Steven Kotler. They turn the commonly held belief that the earth is running out of resources on its head. Rather than perpetuate the fear that the world is dying a slow death, and the population explosion will place ten billion people on the planet by 2050, they offered examples of how the world's scarcity can be turned into abundance.

Diamandis and Kotler write from a secular viewpoint, and admit that there will be catastrophes, wars, and famines. But as I read, my soul resounded that all is not doom and gloom. There are amazing opportunities: a solution for almost every scarcity.

The book is fascinating, and full of optimism not easily seen today. It is not a "feel good" book, but a well-thought-out rationale for how we may deal with the problems of scarcity in the years to come. Simply stated, Diamandis and Kotler espouse the notion that rather than a planet running out of resources, there is reasoned hope (with the right combination of technology, entrepreneurs and human ingenuity) for solving almost every problem confronting us.

"Imagine a world of nine billion people with clean water, nutritious food, affordable housing, personalized education, top-tier medical care, and nonpolluting, ubiquitous energy. Building this better world is humanity's greatest challenge. What follows is the story of how we can rise to meet it."

It didn't require a lot of imagination to apply this principle of abundance to the Ministry Center. There is an irony that the world's population is exploding, and the church's population is imploding.

I think the number one requirement for launching out in faith to start a Ministry Center is to "think abundance". Abundance is all around us; especially the abundance of faith and opportunity.

"...and prove me now herewith, says the LORD of hosts, if I will not open you the windows of heaven, and pour you out a blessing, that there shall not be room enough to receive it!" (Malachi 3:10)

The Communion of Abundance: Water into Wine

Jesus performed his first miracle at the wedding in Cana, changing water to wine. The miracle itself speaks to God's abundance. Jesus filled the pots to overflowing! Add to that the joy this miracle brought to the wedding ceremony and you have enough points for a good sermon. That transforming power is available to us, both as individuals and churches.

Jesus apparently was a great winemaker. The thing that I have overlooked is The WINE Connection between Jesus' first miracle at Cana (water to WINE) and his last act of ministry: breaking bread and sharing WINE with his disciples as his broken body and atoning blood.

Notice the progression:
The Water symbolizes Life; often ordinary and without power.
The Wine symbolizes the Abundant Life, that powerful life Jesus wants each of his children to enjoy.
The Blood symbolizes Eternal Life; an eternity in Communion with our Lord.

The host of the feast, upon tasting the transformed wine, said Jesus had "saved the best to the last". I suspect that is the way Jesus still works. Even for churches, for those who allow Jesus to change our lives from the ordinary to the abundant and eternal, the best is yet to be.

Someone put it this way: *"God pours death into life and life into death without spilling a drop."*

Divine Economy of Abundance

Rev. John Edgar is my kind of minister. What he has done at the Church and Community Development for All People in Columbus, Ohio, a United Methodist church and urban ministry center, is not much different from what happened here at Christ Ministry Center.

He proves the saying: *"The way you see the problem IS the Problem!"*

Too often churches start by looking at needs and deficiencies: what they do not have rather than the unseen abundance all around them; and what they cannot do because of their perceived lack of resources.

"We get so preoccupied with 'there's a need' or 'there is something broken' that we don't realize that achieves absolutely nothing because you can't build anything with nothing," Edgar told a gathering of Minnesota United Methodist faith leaders in October 2015.

Rev. Edgar stopped bemoaning the urban blight and overwhelming needs of his depressed Columbus neighborhood 16 years ago. That's when Edgar rolled up his sleeves and, with the help of seventy-eight Methodist churches in his district, opened a "free store" with donated household items to give away in a rented store front. The idea took hold, and the free store gave out $2 million worth of merchandise in 2014.

Divine economy of abundance

Where I shout a loud "AMEN" is when Edgar teaches the principle of the "divine economy of abundance". For me, this is the essential component for a church or Ministry Center. Call it abundance or optimism, it really just boils down to simple FAITH!

It's biblical, too. Remember the story of how Jesus fed 5,000 with just two fish and five loaves? Linda DiGiorgio (late founder and CEO of Crossroads Ministries that will give away $1 million of groceries here at Christ Ministry Center this year) proved those kinds of miracles still happen.

"God organized creation so there's enough of every good gift that if we use those gifts for God's purposes, we will always have available the assets and the resources that are needed," Edgar asserts.

Scarcity, he adds, is a myth.

"God made it, God made it good, it's abundant, and if we take what we have, no matter how meager it seems to us, God will multiply it and there'll be enough," he said. As proof, Edgar said that there was never a time in the free store's 16-year history when its 7,000 square feet wasn't filled from floor to ceiling.

Asset-based community development

Edgar calls this principle "asset-based community development", which he says will work almost anywhere. Today, in addition to its original free store, Community Development for All People now also includes affordable housing, an after-school program, a clinic, a charitable pharmacy, a bike shop, community gardens, and a healthy eating and living program.

It's the old "glass half empty-half full" paradigm. Every neighborhood has assets and resources. Need-based strategies (the traditional way of viewing a church neighborhood) begin by focusing on crime, broken families, unemployment, child abuse, drop-outs, and other problems. By contrast, asset-based development starts by looking at what's working—such as libraries, parks, public entities, churches, neighborhood block clubs, schools, and colleges—and builds from there.

"I am personally convinced that one of the chronic ailments of United Methodist folks is this sort of paralysis of analysis," Edgar said. *"We're sitting around thinking about stuff and not realizing...getting it done is about assembling assets and resources."*

Identifying assets and championing a common vision
Edgar says if your current efforts aren't producing results, asking the same people who came up with the unsuccessful idea to provide another one doesn't make sense.

Imagine what you could do, he said, if you take these assets and rally around a common goal. "Start small, tell the story, and welcome in partners"—and you can transform lives and communities in huge ways.

"According to your faith, so be it unto you!"

(Many thanks to Christa Meland, director of communications for the Minnesota Annual Conference of the United Methodist Church for sharing Rev. Edgar's story.)

"Two Little Loaves"
I had been struggling to find a way to express abundance. Not the kind of abundance televangelists talk about. You know, "Send me $100 and God will give you $1000 in return". I'm talking about the abundance Jesus talked about: Faith the size off a mustard seed, and how two loaves and five fish can feed 5,000.

As I listened to Linda Di Giorgio's pastor deliver her memorial message, I realized Linda was the living example of what God's abundance means.

Linda never had much of this world's riches. What she had was an enormous faith, a caring heart and an energetic willingness to connect people with food for both their souls and bodies.

Her pastor recalled it all started many years ago when Linda was in a "Day Old Bread" shop in El Cajon. She saw a couple loaves of bread sitting on the counter. She asked the shop manager what those were for and learned they were about to be thrown out. *"Don't throw them away. May I have them?"* she asked. Of course the shop manager said she could take them, free of charge.

Those of us who were blessed to know Linda would not be surprised she immediately drove to the home of a family in need and shared the bread. That's when Crossroads Christian Ministry was born.

Linda realized there must be an abundance of food that gets thrown out every day. She began checking with grocery stores, fast food outlets and even Starbucks. Sure enough, those two loaves became truckloads of perfectly good, but soon-to-expire, food. All she needed were some trucks and volunteers to help her collect and distribute the food.

From those two meager day-old loaves, Crossroads grew into a charity giving away over a million dollars' worth of food every year!

And if you think Linda did it for profit, she never drew a salary. As a matter of fact, she and her husband Bob put far more money into Crossroads than they ever received. Trucks break down, and need expensive repairs. Food handling in California requires all kinds of permits and insurance. Often Linda would buy meats and canned goods to make sure those who came for food assistance didn't "live by bread alone." Her pastor said he knew the Di Giorgio's credit cards were often maxed out just to keep the food ministry going.

Then there were truck drivers who didn't show up, and volunteers who sometimes brought problems from home. Linda was often a minister, counselor and referee. I never saw her angry, even when she had every right to be.

Her pastor used Matthew 25 as the text of his sermon. *"I was hungry, and you gave me something to eat."* Then he continued to the part that says, *"Lord, when did I see you hungry and give you food?"* The reply: *"When you did it to the least of these, you did it unto me."*

That was Linda. She didn't seek praise or acclaim for her acts of kindness. It was just her nature to give bread to the hungry, even if she had to pay for it herself. And that included spiritual food as well. She always gave a smile, a word of encouragement, and God's love with every loaf.

As I looked around the sanctuary at Covenant Presbyterian, Linda's home church, I saw an amazing diversity among the hundred or more who paid their respects: rich and poor; young and old; white, black and Hispanic; Christian and non-believers; citizens, immigrants and refugees; Ph.D.'s and special needs volunteers. Linda didn't discriminate. She loved them all.

Linda had many physical challenges. She managed Crossroads' million-dollar food giveaways from her motorized wheel chair. One of her lead volunteers said he never heard Linda say she was tired. No doubt she was, but the sheer adrenalin and excitement of helping the hungry was greater than her fatigue.

So the next time you start thinking how little you or your church has, remember Linda. If she could take two loaves of day-old bread and create a million-dollar feast, so can anyone. All it takes is faith to open your eyes and see the treasures at your feet, a loving heart, and a willingness to serve God by sharing from his abundant storehouse.

Chapter 11: Can We Really Trust God to Succeed?
(Trusting God)

"In everything you do, put God first, and he will direct you and crown your efforts with success." (Proverbs 3:6, Living Bible)

Success is pretty simple. Simple, but not easy. Of course, all depends on what and how you define success for your church or Ministry Center.

Success for churches has traditionally been measured by "The 4-B's": Buildings, budgets, baptisms and 'bottoms in the pews'. It's a numbers game. If your numbers are increasing, you are a success. If not, then you are failing.

Numbers tell a part of our story. I do not want to ignore what numbers tell us. But when numbers become the goal, it is easy to lose focus upon our vision. Numbers can become a form of idolatry when they become more important than serving our Lord.

Hebrews 11 is called "Faith's Hall of Fame". It recounts how such leaders as Noah, Sarah and Abraham were champions of faith. But by the world's standards, they were total failures.

"Each one of these people of faith died not yet having in hand what was promised, but still believing. How did they do it? They saw it way off in the distance, waved their greeting, and accepted the fact that they were transients in this world. People who live this way make it plain that they are looking for their true home. If they were homesick for the old country, they could have gone back any time they wanted. But they were after a far better country than that—heaven country. You can see why God is so proud of them, and has a City waiting for them." (Hebrews 11:13-16)

Dr. Clyde Francisco, my Old Testament seminary professor, once said, *"God promised Abraham not only that he would have many descendants, but 'I will give the whole land of Canaan to your family forever, and I will be their God.' Yet the only parcel of land Abraham ever 'owned' was deed to the Cave of Machpelah, where be buried his beloved wife, and where he himself was later interred." Did that make Abraham a failure? Of course not."*

This passage states what success looks like for a Ministry Center. Its goal is to make for "a far better country" or a piece of God's Kingdom on earth as it is in heaven. That is not often evident in numbers alone.

I would like to offer some measures of success for a Ministry Center.
- It helps break the chains of injustice
- It eradicates exploitation in the workplace
- It helps set free the oppressed
- It frees debtors their debts
- It shares food with the hungry
- It provides a home for the homeless
- It clothes the ill-clad and shivering

If that sounds familiar and like Matthew 25's Ministry Center Model, you are correct. But this passage comes from Isaiah 58:6-7. It is the Old Testament passage Jesus quoted in the Synagogue.

> *"This is the kind of fast day I'm after:*
> *to break the chains of injustice,*
> *get rid of exploitation in the workplace,*
> *free the oppressed,*
> *cancel debts.*
> *What I'm interested in seeing you do is:*
> *sharing your food with the hungry,*
> *inviting the homeless poor into your homes,*
> *putting clothes on the shivering ill-clad,*
> *being available to your own families." (Isaiah 58:6-7)*

But don't miss what follows!

> *"Do this and the lights will turn on,*
> *and your lives will turn around at once.*
> *Your righteousness will pave your way.*
> *The God of glory will secure your passage.*
> *Then when you pray, God will answer.*
> *You'll call out for help and I'll say, 'Here I am.'" (Isaiah 58:8-9)*

This is what success looks like in a Ministry Center. When you do the will and work of God, the lights will turn on; your lives will turn around at once. God will pave a way for you and grant you safe passage. And best of all, when you call out to God for help, the Great I AM will say *"Here I am."*

Success has little to do with money and numbers. It has everything to do with doing the will of God and achieving your purpose in life. That holds true for churches as well as individuals.

Raymond J. Bakke, urban ministry pioneer, wrote, *"For many years I've struggled to help pastors understand the urban church-growth reality. It just can't be measured by the number of members, people in attendance or dollars in the offering. A city church of 100 can have ten or more countries in the membership. City churches are hubs, "worldwide webs" of relationships that link back to family or colleagues in sending countries where the ministry is underground or mushrooming right now."*

He added, *"With blessing from the Colossian Scriptures, we can mobilize to reform city schools and health-care systems. We can work for justice in the courts of law and demand policies that are fair for all, especially the most vulnerable people in our society. We can engage in all these strategies in the name of our risen and reigning Lord whose kingdom has come, but not in its fullness."*

The church at Philippi was the first church started in Europe. The Apostle Paul wrote that their model of generosity was one all churches should follow. And he added, *"There has never been the slightest doubt in my mind that the God who started this great work in you would keep at it and bring it to a flourishing finish on the very day Christ Jesus appears."* *(Philippians 1:3-6)*

One of the greatest measures of success is, did the person being helped "feel God's love" in the interaction, even if only for a moment? Did he or she see God through you?

So can you succeed, even if you have few resources? Absolutely, yes!

Dr. Wayne Oates on Faith and Anxiety
Perhaps the most remarkable teacher I have ever had was Dr. Wayne Oates, whom many called the "Father of American Clinical Pastoral Care." He coined the term "workaholic".

Born into abject Carolina poverty, abandoned as an infant by his father, Wayne Oates saw faith and education as his pathway out of the chains of poverty and insecurity that bound him.

No more genuinely humble man walked this globe. Dr. Oates, in his simple, yet profound manner, once said in a lecture: *"Some people think the opposite of faith is DOUBT. The opposite of faith is ANXIETY."*

Wayne Oates, the cotton mill child of Greenville, South Carolina, wrote 57 books. I recommend all of them, but especially *"Anxiety in the Christian Experience"*.

Someone said, *"Every tomorrow has two handles. We can take hold of it by the handle of anxiety, or by the handle of faith."* She adds, *"A little faith will bring your soul to heaven, but a lot of faith will bring heaven to your soul."* I think Wayne Oates would agree with that.

Faith in Action
One of the most humbling experiences of my ministry was when I received a call from a single mother who said, *"It worked!"* I asked *"What worked?"* She had responded to my appeal from the pulpit to be faithful in stewardship by placing the last money she had in the offering plate as her tithe to the Lord. It meant she and her daughter had no money for food, gasoline, or anything until her next paycheck, which was over a week away. Before I could say anything, she informed me a large, unexpected check arrived the next day in the mail.

While I would have counseled her, given the opportunity, that I was not suggesting she give her last dollar, she experienced it as an answer to her need. It was, she explained, a blessing for her stepping out in faith to help her church and for being faithful to God in stewardship.

How long has it been since you put your faith into action? How long has it been since you practiced radical faith that could cost you everything? It is when we experience "doing faith" that we abound in faith, hope and love.

SECTION THREE: Ministry Center Assessment

Chapter 12: What Is A "Ministry Center Business Model"?
(Ministering Stewardship)

"The way God designed our bodies is a model for understanding our lives together as a church: every part dependent on every other part, the parts we mention and the parts we don't, the parts we see and the parts we don't. If one part hurts, every other part is involved in the hurt, and in the healing. If one part flourishes, every other part enters into the exuberance." (1 Corinthians 12:25-26)

To truly understand the Ministry Center Business Model, you have to contrast it with the typical Church Business Model.

Business Models
A business model is basically a representation of:
- What you are going to do (mission)
- How you are going to do it (function)
- Who you are doing it for (clientele)
- How you generate revenue (funding)

Typical Church Model
Appendix A is a simple business model of a typical church.
- *The primary focus/mission* is on their congregation, and is usually about making them better Christians.
- *The primary revenue* is offerings from their congregation. As the church gets past its prime, and older/grayer; the congregation tends to dwindle – and so does the central revenue stream. *(This may be where you are now.)*

The Ministry Center Model
The Ministry Center Model is not such a radical departure from the typical church model. It *tweaks the mission and revenue streams* – but ultimately part of its mission is still providing religious education and worship, the same as in the typical church model.

Appendix B shows the Ministry Center Model.

The *focus (mission) has broadened,* to not only include religious education and worship, but to minister to physical needs as well (food, clothing, shelter, etc.). The *revenue has shifted* to primarily rental incomes.

What this change accomplishes is to cause the churches and charities *to pay you* (via rent) to perform the "good works" of Matthew 25, that you want achieved. Partners also do this work for you for free.

Advantages:
- Your mission is broader, thereby serving more people
- You do not bear the expenses or headaches of having a large staff to manage – each church or charity manages their own staff
- You have more revenue to maintain your building
- The revenue stream is more stable and predictable than offerings
- You can still help your legacy congregation to succeed

Disadvantages:
- You don't have "control" over your renters or their programs *(other than evicting them)*
- There is probably a lot more "management" for you than you may expect

Business Model in Action
When I started Christ Ministry Center, I wasn't really aware that was what I was doing. All I knew was that God was urging me to not only tend His flock, but reminding me that I had a large building at my disposal which was woefully underutilized.

Prior to my assignment to Christ Church, there was already one Hispanic church who rented space there, and also the first floor was exclusively used by a daycare center that the last Pastor had founded. Things were not right with that daycare. The workers were not respectful of the church building or the congregants, or of God either. They thought that they were the most important thing happening in the building and they had started making all the decisions about the church, from the circus colors that the interior was painted, to what hours the building would be opened and closed, and who could enter the building while they were there. They were paying $800/month rent to the church, and the church had been clinging to that meager income for several years, believing it was the only thing standing between them and closing the church doors.

As the new Pastor, I didn't feel it was right making changes on day one, but after several weeks of viewing how the daycare was operating, and the insolent, disrespectful behavior of the workers, I spoke with their Director, and told her some changes were going to have to be made if they were to stay. Basically I was told in no uncertain terms that I didn't make the rules, they did. Against the advice of my church Finance Committee and Trustees, I evicted them.

I didn't have a plan for how we were going to replace that lost income, but I stepped out on faith that it was the right thing to do, and that "the Lord will provide." I asked the congregation and especially my wife, to fix up the spaces that had been abandoned, because they were filthy and in disrepair. Amidst the "Armageddon" mutterings going on around me, I was confident that we were preparing for something "better".

Shortly after that, an organization that had connections to the Methodist denomination contacted me and asked if we had any office spaces they could lease to operate their social ministry organization. They rented the entire second floor!

The Ministry Center was born – but I still didn't realize it. I kept working on ideas and plans about bolstering up the Church, even as it dwindled and the offerings were not close to keeping the doors open, much less making desperately needed deferred building repairs.

The large social ministry organization moved on after several years and I again heard from the naysayers about us closing the doors. But other organizations showed up at our door. Just like manna for the Israelites, we always had enough income to "survive" but not thrive (yet!). I thought I was buying time until the congregation could become powerful enough to support the building, but God kept whispering in my ear to open my eyes and see the future.

Finally, the epiphany: I felt the right thing was not to keep trying to resurrect the church, but to use the resources God had placed in my trust for a "Ministry Center". And I never looked back.

It wasn't until years later that my wife pointed out to me the "Business Model" of the Ministry Center, and I saw the simplicity and genius of it. I never could have imagined this by myself and I would say that I stumbled into it – but I know I had a divine impetus. To God goes the glory!

Fossils and Lizards: The Church in Creative Tension

Dr. Bruce Birch, Dean of Wesley Theological Seminary in Washington DC, stated the church lives in the *"creative tension of memory and vision"*. He cited many Old Testament prophets, quoting such verses as *"Forget not the rock from which you are hewn"* and, *"Where there is no vision, the people perish"*. This illustrates the tension the people of God have always faced.

First, there is the tendency for the church to live in the past, celebrating her memories, but having no vision of the future. Such a church is like a fossil, Birch said. *"A fossil is an amazingly consistent witness to the past, but totally incapable of dynamic ministry in the present or future."* Many churches today have become fossilized.

In the movie based upon the book by the same name, *"A Man Called Peter"*, young Dr. Peter Marshall preached his first sermon at the New York Avenue Presbyterian Church in Washington DC. The church was virtually dead, but the handful of remaining members proudly showed their new pastor the roped off "Abraham Lincoln Pew" where the great President once sat while attending worship. Dr. Marshall helped that church move from "fossil" to a new vision of what it means to minister in the setting where God placed them; totally engaged in their community in the present tense.

Secondly, there is the tendency for the church to live in the future. Such a church is like a chameleon, becoming all things to all people, but having no roots in the rich traditions of the Bible and church experience. Like the lizard that changes its color to reflect its environment, the church may become irrelevant in its witness to the eternal truths entrusted to her.

Neither model alone is sufficient. The church with a healthy balance between "memory" and "vision" will be able to not only survive, but remain effective in her mission and ministry, regardless of the changing tides of time.

Finding the healthy balance between lizards and fossils comes as we dream a new dream, and get a new glimpse of the vision where God is leading us while we claim a wonderful, rich history.

"What you need to know about the past is that no matter what has happened, it has all worked together to bring you to this very moment. And this is the moment you can choose to make everything new. Right now." ~ Author Unknown

Chapter 13: How to Assess If This Is for Us?
(Assessing Self)

"It is clear to us, friends, that God not only loves you very much but also has put his hand on you for something special. When the Message we preached came to you, it wasn't just words. Something happened in you. The Holy Spirit put steel in your convictions." (1 Thessalonians 1:2-5)

Once you have taken an honest look at your church, determined who "owns the church", and discerned God's leadership to become a Ministry Center, the next step is to make objective assessments that will give you empirical data to make the final decision and commitment.

This chapter offers some of those self-assessments with guidelines for conducting them.

Self-Assessment: Who Are You?

The poet Robert Burns wrote, *"...to see ourselves as others see us."* Remember the first time you heard your own voice on a tape recording? Or, remember when you first saw yourself in a home video? In denial, we tend to say, *"That's not me!"* But that is how others see and hear us.

Chapter 6 dealt with church ownership. The self-assessment goes a step further in defining who you are as a church. Both are necessary in becoming a Ministry Center.

Churches are no different from humans when it comes to looking in the mirror. We have a self-image and assume the neighborhood shares that perspective. Most likely, they see something different. That accounts for the disconnection between church and community. They don't "get it", and we don't understand why they don't get it. So it behooves a church, especially a struggling church, to take an honest look at itself.

We tend to not see the cobwebs near the ceiling or coffee stains in the carpet. We assume everyone knows where the sanctuary and social hall are, not to mention the restrooms or church office.

For instance, ask a trusted friend to come to your church for their first time. Let them know it is not an attempt to "evangelize" them, but to give you some candid feedback. Ask them to share their honest impressions. Those include their first impression of your church's "curb appeal". Next, did they find well marked signage to direct them to places in your building? If it is during a worship service, what impressions did they get? Were they greeted appropriately (not too strongly, but certainly not ignored)?

Perhaps you have already done an evaluation of your building, worship style and surveyed the neighborhood. Maybe you have altered your music and worship time and added social media. Yet it may not have increased participation in worship and church life.

This book is not how to find a gimmick to fill the pews and offering plates. Oddly, we found that by not seeking a goal of "full pews and full offering plates", more people than ever now enter our doors. And God has provided the funds to both minister to our community and maintain our aging facilities.

This book provides several assessments to help you take an honest and candid look at where you have been, where you now are, and where you are going. It encourages you to rethink church and find a new inspiration and role in your community and in the Kingdom of God.

Vision Statement versus Mission Statement
While a mission statement defines what an organization is and why it exists, a vision statement describes what that organization looks like at least five years in the future.

Vision Assessment: Where Are You Going?
The Bible says, *"Where there is no vision, the people perish." (Proverbs 29:18)*. The first assessment is when *"your young men will see visions; your old men will dream dreams." (Joel 2:28)*. Many churches, especially the older ones, have lost sight of their vision. As times have changed, the original vision has not kept pace and is now outdated or even irrelevant. It's time to dream a new, bold and exciting dream for your church.

Begin with the Goal in Mind
Steven Covey stated in his "*7 Habits of Highly Effective People*", you should have a vision of where you are going. Without a goal, you do not know where you are going, how to get there, or even when you arrive. So begin your discernment with a goal in mind. It may be a bit foggy now, but it will become clearer as you walk by faith toward God's will for your church. And remember, just keeping the lights on and the doors open is not a valid vision for a Ministry Center.

Imagine
You have to understand your former mission and vision for your church and imagine a new vision and mission.

Facing Up to Fear
One impediment to move from church to Ministry Center is fear: the fear of the unknown and the fear of failure.

In the Greek, the word for fear is *phobos* from which we get our word "phobia". Psychologists will tell you that phobias are "irrational fears" rooted in the sense that one has "lost control" and cannot deal with the potential (but almost never realized) consequences. Bullies have been using fear for a long time.

Surrendering to fear never succeeds. That is true whether dealing with Barbarians or your own phobias. As FDR said, *"We have nothing to fear but fear itself."*

Fear is powerful. It has a paralyzing effect. It is at the root of the survivalist movement, where people have abandoned their normal lives to stock up supplies in underground bunkers so they can "survive" the apocalypse (always 'just around the corner'). In the meantime, they forfeit living the healthy, productive life God gave them as they succumb to their worst fears.

Fear produces cowards. Courage produces leaders.

Not all fears are irrational. Fear is a legitimate primal emotion given to us by God to alert us to imminent danger. We should not ignore it. But we must also not be ruled by fears.

The list of things over which you might be fearful is endless. Whether it is fear for your family, health, job, money, relationships, death, or (in your extended world) fear of the economy, environment, or world tyrants, you don't have to look far to find something that can paralyze you with fear.

Fear is a spiritual matter. Fear destroys hope. Put another way, fear is putting your faith into believing the worst things will happen.

Solomon understood this. In Proverbs 28:1 he wrote, *"The wicked are edgy with guilt, ready to run off even when no one's after them; Honest people are relaxed and confident, bold as lions."*

So much of our precious short lives are wasted on fearing things that never come to pass.

So what is the antidote to fear? You might be surprised, it is LOVE. In 1 John 4:16-18, we read: *"God is love…There is no fear in love [dread does not exist], but full-grown (complete, perfect) love turns fear out of doors and expels every trace of terror! For fear brings with it the thought of punishment, and [so] he (or she) who is afraid has not reached the full maturity of love [is not yet grown into love's complete perfection]."* (Amplified Bible)

To live in fear (or not) is a choice. You alone are in control of that decision. But with the help of God, *"perfect love will cast out fear"*.

Chapter 14: What Should We Do as A Ministry Center?
(Assessing Needs)

"He comes alongside us when we go through hard times, and before you know it, he brings us alongside someone else who is going through hard times so that we can be there for that person just as God was there for us. We have plenty of hard times that come from following the Messiah, but no more so than the good times of his healing comfort—we get a full measure of that, too." (2 Corinthians 1:3-5)

After looking at yourself, then decide what you need to do.

Your Vision and Mission Statements
A vision statement identifies where you are going. The mission statement defines how you will get there.

Don't think a mission (purpose) statement is only for a business. It is for any organization to clearly define and understand who they are and why they exist. If an organization has no goals or purpose, what is the point of their being? If an organization doesn't understand its core purpose, then it seldom achieves it, and their actions are scattered rather than focused.

First look at your current mission, what is it? Most churches have a mission something along the lines of *"spreading the word of the gospel"*; *"making disciples"*; *"leading people to Christ"*; *"saving souls"* or some combination of those concepts. Is your current mission the same mission you want to continue? Do your members know your mission statement? Is it helping you achieve your goal? If so, why consider changing it? But as a Ministry Center – or whatever you want to call yourself in the future – what would your purpose (mission) be? What do you want to be doing differently that you aren't doing now? Perhaps you want to include your old mission and just supplement that with what you want to do in the future. Or perhaps you want an entirely new mission/purpose. You do not have to get a mission statement entirely polished at this point, but you want to have a clear vision of what you want to be doing differently than you are now and get that into words.

A mission (or purpose) statement is short and defines what an organization is, and why it exists, which is its reason for being. At a minimum, your mission statement should define who your primary "clientele" are (who you are going to serve), and identify the services (in general terms) you will provide.

As an example, here is the mission statement of Christ Ministry Center (CMC) San Diego:

"The purpose of Christ United Methodist Ministry Center is to:
- Provide a nurturing environment for worship, religious education and fellowship for religious congregations in the advancement of religion and ministry;
- Provide a base of operations for charitable and community non-profit organizations engaged in public benefit ministries; especially relief of the poor, distressed and underprivileged;
- Create and maintain a mechanism to harness the resources of existing non-profit charities and churches in the San Diego area which enables them more efficiency and effectiveness in helping the helpless."

Notice this mission statement includes WHY we exist; WHO we serve; and WHAT services we provide. It is the jumping off point for everything that follows.

CMC continues to explain (but not as part of the mission statement) how we achieve our purposes: "by offering a home for 'homeless congregations' to worship and minister; and for public benefit charities to 'relieve the poor and distressed'" (that explains the first two bullets above). "Plus, by providing **The Fount of Blessings** (My Fount.com) we help churches, charities and social agencies (both public and private) to become more efficient and effective in meeting the needs of the poor" (which explains how we achieve our third bullet's purpose). See Chapter 27 for more on the Fount of Blessings.

Identify Future Services You Want to Provide
Each step builds on the previous step. Once God has led you to see a new vision and purpose for your existing church, then you need to clearly identify what services you are being called to in your new mission. For example, Christ Ministry Center uses the model of Matthew 25:35-37 to focus their Ministry: *"I was hungry, thirsty, naked, sick, a stranger, in prison..."* Therefore, our Ministry Center's helping services were designed to meet those particular needs.

In Chapter 5, we defined "thirsty" as "spiritual thirst" (like the woman at the well). The dozen congregations who share our worship spaces fulfill this need by providing religious services, education, fellowship, counseling and outreach. Likewise, we identify being "a stranger" to encompass helping the diverse population who recently arrived in our community. In urban areas, churches and Ministry Centers can "go ye into all the world" by traveling just a few blocks. Increasingly the world is literally at our doorstep. To ignore the strangers in our midst is to miss one of the greatest opportunities for revitalizing our churches. "In prison" was interpreted to not only minister to those in a literal prison or recently released, but to help those people who are in a "self-imposed prison" of addictions, such as gambling, drugs, alcohol, pornography, etc. CMC provides spaces for a number of twelve step groups such as Alcoholics Anonymous (AA), Narcotics Anonymous (NA), and Gambling Recovery Ministries; and is home to one or more charities who serve those recently released from prison.

You don't necessarily have to provide a wide variety of ministries and services; perhaps you are being called to fulfill only a few different needs, or conceivably only one. Some urban churches are in locations where unemployment is very high among the most vulnerable groups of young people, which leads to many other problems. A church could easily devote all or most of their spaces just in training these youths toward getting jobs. The services God has led you to provide should usually (but not always) be consistent with the needs in your area.

You should already have a pretty good idea of what needs there are in your community from the people who have come to your church seeking help. It could be shelter, medical services, mental health services, general poverty, food, unemployment, etc.

In Chapter 27, I explain how "The Fount" could work for you, and enable you to help most anyone find what they need in your local area.

Look at ministries being provided now and you may want to just expand on that need. Or perhaps there were ministries that you always wanted to perform but couldn't due to a lack of resources. Make your selections based on a "new organization" not what you have the capacity to provide now. Your focus and thinking should shift away from just serving your current congregation or trying to attract more people to your current services. You are asking God to direct you to how he could use your organization in the future.

Some "formerly one denomination churches" may have a calling to provide a "home" for new churches. Many churches feel that because their membership has grown old and is dying off and they can't attract enough new members that a church could not survive in their location. That may or may not be true. Maybe their neighborhood has undergone a transition and their neighbors are of a different denomination, ethnicity, or age group and they are looking for a "different" church than what you have previously provided.

It is even possible that you could become a home for one or more charities that don't have a local mission at all. A charity might be looking for office space, staging areas, or work spaces in your city, but are serving an orphanage overseas, or are a chapter of a national or worldwide charitable organization.

Identify Those Who May Need These Services (your future clientele)
There are several aspects to this. It is not enough to hear the calling and identify *how* you can serve, but in practical terms, you have to assess and access the pool of persons to be served. For example, if you felt called to provide a food ministry, are you located geographically in a place where the majority of the underfed can even access you?

If you are not located in an area that your clientele can reach you, then that is going to be a problem. It is not necessarily insurmountable, but you would have to solve the problem of whether "Mohammed goes to the mountain, or the mountain comes to Mohammed".

There may be some service you want to offer that already has a specifically identified group you are trying to reach, such as "providing clothes to children in your local homeless shelter". That need should be readily quantifiable by talking with the group that runs the homeless shelter and getting information on how many children are usually there, and what type of clothes they need most. That will help you refine what you need to provide in order to achieve that particular purpose

However, initially, you need to have some assurance that there are "customers" (clientele) for the service(s) you want to provide. In larger cities, where there are enormous needs, you might consider limiting the pool of prospective clientele (such as to your neighborhood or in your city) to keep it manageable; although most organizations seldom turn away anyone truly in need, and rather instead try to increase their capacity to fill the needs.

Assess the Spiritual and Emotional Climate of Your Current Congregation

If you have a current congregation, you have to meet with them to discern how they feel and what they want for their church, and it is likely you have already had this meeting(s). Generally, what they want is for the glory days to return and to be a robust church again and to relive the successful times of the past. If you are an old church, many of the congregants may be quite elderly. You need to talk with them even though it is probably going to be painful and upsetting for them. You want to be as gentle as possible, but you have to explain to them why things are not going well enough to continue the status quo, and that you are thinking out of the box about what the future might hold.

Naturally their real concern is "how does this affect me?" There are a number of options here and this is so preliminary at this stage that you may want to avoid this part of the conversation for the present and defer it with some statement that it hasn't really been that thought out yet—which is true. But even though this is a disturbing topic to them, you have to talk to them instead of avoiding them, because the rumor mill will easily get ahead of you. Bad news is better than no news, and integrity demands that you do not go silent on them if you actually might be planning to head down a dramatically converted path.

However, in reality you have to seriously be thinking about what would/could happen to your legacy congregation (if you have one), in the eventuality you go to a completely different type of purpose/organizational structure. The possibilities for a legacy congregation are not endless here, and they usually fall in one of two broader categories: either their opportunity to worship in their same building will continue in some fashion, or it won't. This doesn't have to mean they are shut down entirely, they could be transferred to a nearby same denomination church for example.

In CMC, the small legacy congregation (less than 20 in worship) was allowed to continue worshipping in the church building, but with a Lay Leader instead of the full Elder that they previously had. There was a retired minister among the small congregation and she administered the sacraments to them, or the previous Elder would occasionally return and serve communion. Theoretically, this change gave them an opportunity to grow their church in the future (which was unlikely for the same reasons they dwindled to the remnant of what they had become), but at a minimum, provided these elderly members a chance to worship in their familiar surroundings until they pass to their greater glory.

(Little did we know that God had a third option for them, which you can read about in Chapter 28.)

The Genuine Good Samaritan
In 2005, Bishop T. D. Jakes of the Potter's House delivered a powerful sermon at Washington's National Cathedral as our nation observed a National Day of Prayer for the victims of Hurricane Katrina. Bishop Jakes used the story of the Good Samaritan as the setting for measuring responses to the wounded and helpless. That wonderful message contained five basic ideas which form an excellent model for how a Ministry Center ministers.

The Levite and the priest teach us that **restoration is more than observation**. These religious leaders saw the man in need, but passed by on the other side, offering no help; pretending he was not there; keeping to their tight schedule; and saying, "Someone else can help him." We see the wounded and helpless all around us. Will the church pass by on the other side of the road?

Real ministry is willing to **reach beyond our neighborhoods**. Jesus told the story of the Good Samaritan in response to a question about "who is my neighbor?" That gets to the heart of the law and prophets, for the greatest "laws" are to love God and my neighbor as myself. If I neatly define my neighbors as people like me, and whom I like, then the task is easy. But for a Samaritan to love a Jew, that takes courage!

To help those beaten down, we must **get off our high horses**. The Samaritan got off his horse, and got down to where the wounded man lay. Jakes said, *"Until we love enough to trade places with the poor...then healing will not be real."* He added, *"You cannot help people if you exult yourself above them."*

Resources, not rhetoric, changed this man's life. Jakes reminded us that in no instance does the Samaritan speak to the wounded man. No blaming, no sermonizing, no pontificating about how he got himself in this situation. No words, just deeds, binding up wounds, healing, and genuine ministry. Good sounding promises are fine; but the proof will be in actions, not words.

Finally, **relationships are productive.** The fact that the Samaritan knew, and held the respect, of the inn keeper, created a hospital for the wounded man. Note also that the Samaritan paid for his care. Ministry always costs us something, or it is not genuine.

Bishop Jakes added these five points are like five fingers on our hands, poised to *"stretch out and touch the hurting, the poor, and the underserved. We cannot multiply by dividing. We cannot add by subtracting."*

Chapter 15: How Much Does It Cost?
(Assessing Finances)

"Just think—you don't need a thing; you've got it all! All God's gifts are right in front of you as you wait expectantly for our Master Jesus to arrive on the scene for the Finale. And not only that, but God himself is right alongside to keep you steady and on track until things are all wrapped up by Jesus. God, who got you started in this spiritual adventure, shares with us the life of his Son and our Master Jesus. He will never give up on you. Never forget that." (1Corinthians 1:7-9)

This chapter looks at three different aspects of cost: (1) What it is costing now; (2) Projected future organizational costs; and (3) What the conversion costs. Only the first is based on actual numbers, but (2) and (3) are going to be based on speculation.

Conversion Costs
A church may become a Ministry Center for little or no cash outlay. Christ Ministry Center spent $7,000 for legal advice and help in filing legal and tax documents, and an $800 filing fee with the Secretary of State. Whatever you decide, make sure you are properly organized and in compliance with both the Internal Revenue Service, state, county and city regulations.

Christ Ministry Center is completely self-sustaining financially. When CMC was Christ Church, we were mostly dependent on dwindling dollars in the offering plate. United Methodist churches are obligated to meet certain financial requirements. These included apportionments (each church's "fair share" of the conference and global church budgets) and minimum standards for clergy salary, housing and insurance. In becoming a Ministry Center, we were no longer required to contribute to conference apportionments and were free to set staff salaries.

If any of my Methodist colleagues read the last paragraph and decide to become a Ministry Center based upon release from apportionments, you will fail. Not only is that the wrong basis for becoming a Ministry Center, it is a breach of trust in our connectional system. Plus, it is a two-edged sword. A Ministry Center that "goes it alone" will find it costs as much, if not more, than the apportionments to find building insurance, liability insurance, health insurance, workers compensation, and a dozen big ticket budget items that are provided by the conference group policies.

Christ Ministry Center went to extraordinary effort to insure we maintained our connection to The United Methodist Church.

There is no paragraph in our Book of Discipline that addresses creating a Ministry Center. It was an extraordinary act of trust between the church, district and conference to step out in faith. In the same resolution that declared the "discontinuance" of Christ United Methodist Church, the California Pacific Annual Conference created Christ United Methodist Ministry Center and passed the charter from CUMC to CMC. (See Appendix C for the Resolution of Discontinuance.)

Another aspect of conversion costs may be if your building needs significant repair or reconfiguration of spaces to facilitate the new model.

Current Costs and Revenues
The good news and the bad news: the revenue needed to run the church versus a Ministry Center differs measurably (although both should be self-supporting and sustainable), but the Ministry Center may have more options for revenue. That is good news if you are financially upside down at the church (spending more than you are receiving), because you could get "right-side up" (CMC righted itself!). But the bad news might be if your chosen leadership has absolutely no business or entrepreneurial attributes. While a Ministry Center is *not* a business because it does not have to "show a profit", it does need to pay all its expenses and put aside a little for huge repairs and unexpected costs. That takes both some business and financial acumen.

Always remember though, that the objective is not just to stay in operation; the objective is to make a tangible difference in people's lives, so sometimes you will have to make the spiritual choices even though it is not the best financial choice.

Having said the cost and revenue of the current church differs significantly from your new organization, there is still value in compiling it, because (1) it forces you to take a realistic look at your current financial situation, (2) it can predict how long you can financially survive while you are putting the new model in place, (3) some of the current expenses and revenue will be applicable to the new organization; and (4) it may show that you are absolutely in no financial position to start a Ministry Center *(for example if you need $1M just to get the building habitable from a safety standpoint)*.

You should probably have a great deal of financial data available to you on your current operations, so it shouldn't take a tremendous amount of effort to compile.

You need to look at how much money you have coming in now, and where it comes from. You also need to review your current expenses (costs) and what that entails (who you are paying and for what). Some of the revenue and the expenses will continue and some will not. Annotate any incomes which are a "one time" revenue or cost. Appendix D provides a format that could assist you. *(Although this Appendix is based on an annual comparison, it is better if you compile the current revenue and expenses on a monthly basis first, and then roll it up into an annual figure. That way you may gain more insight into any current financial difficulties you have; which in turn, may affect your future decisions.)*

Future Revenue Streams
Most churches looking to convert to a Ministry Center don't generally have a lot of resources, either financially or otherwise. It requires revenue to run a Ministry Center, so you have to be financially attuned and astute whether you want to or not. A substantial part of whether you can successfully operate a Ministry Center hinges on whether you have sufficient revenue streams. (See the Business Models in Appendices A and B.)

You should have a pretty good idea of your future organization from the work you have done so far in identifying potential services, potential clientele, and envisioning your new mission. What will change in your new world? Look at your current revenue streams (where your money comes from) and identify which ones would no longer exist in the new organization. Deduct those from your future planned revenue. Then envision what new revenues the new organization might involve. Rents? Grants? Fund Raisers? Endowments? Sale of property or assets no longer needed? Identify those and annotate which are 'one time revenues' and which are 'recurring revenues'. Add the new recurring revenues to your list of future revenue. (Note that some of the one-time revenues may be used to help finance conversion/start-up costs. Sales of 50-year-old silver tea services; pews that were removed to provide handicapped access; and old unused pianos generated some one-time revenues that were used in the conversion of CMC.)

Staffing Costs

You are going to have to review your current staff. Personnel are generally always your highest cost in any budget. Envision the new organization and what kind of staff that would involve. Right now you don't have to make the really hard decisions – as to whether or not any of your current staff could transition into the roles needed for the future staff. For the time being, you just have to identify how many staff positions are needed for the future organization and what type they would be (i.e., Director, administrative assistance, financial, custodial, etc.); and how much that would cost.

Remember, that depending on how you are expecting to handle your legacy congregation (if that applies), is going to have a tremendous impact on your financial assessment. Because if you have decided they will not continue as part of the new organization, then you should eliminate the revenue stream derived from that congregation's offerings in your future planning. On the other hand, if they are not going to be part of your new organization, then you should no longer have the cost burden of positions associated with their congregation such as minister(s), musical staff, etc. However, if they continue to worship in the building but are separate from your new organization and will retain their own offerings, then it is appropriate for them to pay their own ministers and musical positions, and also to pay a rental fee as you would charge any other tenant. That rental fee should be included in your new future revenue stream planning. It is appropriate to charge the congregation rent because you will have taken the cost burden off of their shoulders for utilities, building maintenance and so forth (which your new organization will be assuming). You want to always treat everyone fairly and look for the win-win solutions.

Tenant/ Partnership Revenue

Identify any groups or partners that you may have now or intend to enlist to provide those future services.

Certainly if you have tenants or partners already in your building, you need to see how they fit into your new direction, even if it is only to retain them for revenue purposes and they are not directly supporting your new vision other than financially. If you plan on obtaining new tenants, either as partners in your new vision, or simply for the sake of revenue, be sure to include that in the revenue streams for the future vision. Many times churches have multiple cell tower tenants simply because they take up little space, don't cause daily problems, and they pay well. There is no sin in using honest commercial sources to financially enable you to support your new mission, but in some cases, it may raise your annual property tax.

The difference to you between a "tenant" and a "partner" involves whether they pay you for spaces or not. Tenants are usually other churches, schools, or charities that rent space from you. Partners are a little more nebulous, and can be groups or organizations that don't pay you, but you allow them to use your spaces because you support their cause(s); or you sit on their Board; or they provide you some type of help; or you provide them some type of help, or even provide them financial assistance. Obviously you are a big fan of whatever they are doing in the name of The Lord and want to have an association with them that helps them and you to fulfill your respective missions.

You have to think about what partners or tenants you don't have now that you would need to recruit to fulfill your new mission.

Sometimes a church may think they know how they best can serve, or want to serve, but do not know how to attract the organizations, partners, tenants, or revenue to make it happen. Word of mouth will be your best help. Your clientele alone will spread the word about how you are helping, both to others needing help and organizations that are providing help. If you have formed some 'strategic alliances' with other groups or organizations (Chapter 9), then they will probably also refer groups to you who are seeking a site.

I am here to testify that *"with God, all things are possible"*. I am always amazed by the opportunities that the Lord sends. He constantly has people and groups I never knew existed, walk through my door and provide a new means for helping the children of God and supporting the Ministry Center. Keep your mind and heart open and God will send what you need.

Debt

You are pretty much stuck with your current debts unless you have some plan on how to quickly eradicate it, such as selling off a parsonage. So debt is considered a "wash" cost (a cost that you have whether you stay as you are, or whether you evolve to a new organization). If you are making regular payments on your debt, such as a Home Equity Line of Credit (HELOC), then the monthly payments would be brought over to the finances of the new Ministry Center as a recurring monthly cost until paid off.

Additionally, include information on any financial assets you have now (bank accounts, investments, trusts, or other types of financial assets you can access), because that goes into the decision making process.

Compare

On Appendix D, you can do a rough comparison of what your current year has cost compared to the first 'established' year of the Ministry Center. *(By 'established', that will probably be the second full year of operation as a Ministry Center, because you likely will not have found your partners/tenants on day one of the conversion.)*

Understand this is quick and dirty, and an extremely simplistic financial comparison; with 50% of it based on an imaginary future organization that at this point is total conjecture.

Churches in urban areas will likely find it easier to obtain partners and tenants than more rural areas. But if you can't envision where/how you could obtain revenue, or how you could make this concept work, then it is unlikely that you have the wherewithal to make this change.

The Real Cost

I have had my share of "out of money experiences". Growing up on Graball Hill in Yazoo City, Mississippi, I didn't realize I was poor until I learned what other people had. Therein is the problem: we measure our wealth by what other people have, not what is inside us!

My Father often said, *"I may not have a dime, but I have a 'million-dollar' family"*. (In honesty, he hastened to say, *"But I wouldn't give you a plug nickel for another one."*) That was a "spoken blessing" to my siblings and me. It taught us that in spite of our lack of earthly possessions, we were Yazoo City's richest family when it came to things money cannot buy: love, family, faith, happiness and health.

John Wesley said, *"When I have money, I get rid of it quickly, lest it find a way into my heart."* Rather than one owning possessions, the possessions have a way of owning the person. When I was pastor in Georgia, a family donated a 27-foot boat to the church. I discovered why they donated it. We, like the donors, sank more money and time into trying to fix up that wreck than it was worth, and eventually gave it away.

Ralph Waldo Emerson reminded us, *"The greatest man in history was the poorest."* Jesus instructed his disciples to travel lightly, and not encumber themselves with earthly possessions.

The truth is: The wealthiest person is not the one who has the most, but the one who needs the least! The real measure of your wealth is how much you'd be worth if you lost all your money!

All that is to say for your church to become a Ministry Center, it is not so much how much money you have in the bank. You have all you need within you. It's called faith!

"God will supply"

"But I have received everything in full and have an abundance; I am amply supplied, having received from Epaphroditus what you have sent, a fragrant aroma, an acceptable sacrifice, well-pleasing to God. And my God will supply all your needs according to His riches in glory in Christ Jesus." (Philippians 4:18-19)

It is a miracle that from day one, Christ Ministry Center has been completely self-supporting. Oh yes, there have been some touch and go days. Churches and charities move in and out. So the budget is forever changing, month to month.

It is natural that I would be anxious when one of our "anchor" ministries moved out, usually because they had outgrown our facilities. We were self-sustaining, but that means we have a barely break-even budget. Even a small partner's exit can make the difference between ending the month in the red or black.

But God taught me a great lesson that has cured my anxiety over finances.

I received a call from a congregation seeking a place to worship. At that time, we were pretty much booked up. Two churches used the sanctuary on Sunday morning and three other churches used it Sunday afternoon and evening. Like a Catholic church with Masses every two hours, we only had a narrow window, 3:00-5:00 p.m. open.

As I talked with the pastor on the other end of the phone, I told him it was unlikely we could accommodate his congregation. But just for sure, I asked him what time was ideal for his worship. *"We would love to find a place to worship between 3:00 and 5:00 on Sunday afternoons,"* he said.

It was at that moment I realized it was not my job to worry about partners. God has and continues to bring just the right organizations at the right time to complete our mission. That is, as long as we remain faithful (full of faith) that this is all God's doing, lest any man should boast.

Chapter 16: Is Our Building Adequate?
(Assessing Facilities & Capacity)

"Jesus then left the Temple. As he walked away, his disciples pointed out how very impressive the Temple architecture was. Jesus said, "You're not impressed by all this sheer size, are you? The truth of the matter is that there's not a stone in that building that is not going to end up in a pile of rubble." (Matthew 24:1-2)

Some of you may be able to imagine your building as a "pile of rubble" more easily than others. One of the things you have to consider in becoming a Ministry Center is your current facility. Does it match with the mission you have identified? There are a number of reasons it may not match.

Size
Maybe your facilities are too small to accomplish the new mission. This may or may not be a showstopper (a block to further progress). Think out of the box: is there another church or charity in your neighborhood you could partner with to fulfill your planned mission? Can your denomination assist you with making available some space in one of their properties? Are there spaces you could rent? Could people in the congregation volunteer spaces in their home or garage? Could you scale down your vision to fit your space? Could you take a different approach as to the *method of how* you provide some service that would take less space?

Style
Do you have enough square footage but it doesn't fit what you want to use it for? For example, you need several big classrooms but all you have are numerous small rooms? Or vice versa? Could you remodel (financially and structurally) into a fit for your vision? Can you alter the vision to fit your existing configuration? Is there another church or charity in your neighborhood with whom you could partner? Can your denomination assist you with making available some space? Could you take a different approach as to the *method of how* you provide some service that would fit your current space? Be sure you consider and assess all of your buildings including parsonages or off site buildings or storage,

Condition
Does the current condition of your building support what you want to use it for? Is it even feasible to think about making necessary repairs (financially and time wise) for such things as a new roof? Cost out what it would take

to get necessary repairs made to evaluate whether it should or could even be done. Also think about whether you have, or could have, termites; lead; asbestos, black mold; etc., and what the remediation would cost.

Improvements
It is not just repairs that you have to think about. Think about what you want to use each space for. If your building is old you probably are going to need some things you currently don't have such as more electrical circuits and panels or computer drops, or air conditioning or new heating.

Parking
Do you have sufficient parking to match your vision? This doesn't necessarily have to be a showstopper. When CMC became the home for a dozen different overlapping congregations and there was insufficient parking on Sundays, they made a partnership agreement with a commercial complex a block away to use their parking lot on Sundays (when those businesses were not open). In return CMC lets those small businesses use conference rooms in the Ministry Center during weekdays when they were normally not in use. And don't forget the repair and condition of the parking lot when making your facility assessment.

Geography
This was mentioned briefly in an earlier assessment on reflecting about who your clientele would be. Ideally you would be conveniently located near where your clients could easily get to you. If you are not, then it will require some creative thinking on your part as to how to overcome that barrier to your success. Geography is also part of the problem that might exist for a country versus city church when it comes to converting to a new mission. It is generally going to be easier for an urban church to make this type of transition, simply because the urban environment holds more, and more varied, opportunities to help people than a small town church. The needs of large inner cities are usually far greater than less populous areas, so the opportunity to help is also far greater. But this may not hold true for every aspect of helping services. It has been shocking how drug use has spread through smaller towns in the last few years. So even in a less populous area The Lord may be leading you to provide a treatment or rehabilitation facility in your future, or even something as simple as a home for Narcotics Anonymous (NA) groups to meet.

Building Codes and Laws
The older your facilities are, the less likely they are to meet building codes. There are ADA (Americans with Disabilities Act) codes *(such as access to*

ramps, restrooms, etc.), electrical codes, plumbing codes, parking codes, etc., and don't forget all the health codes for food preparation facilities. It is possible that you are currently grandfathered under the old codes, but if you remodel in any way you may be subject to meeting the new codes. Also if you are planning to start something like a shelter for the homeless or for battered women, you might need to check on whether your building is zoned for that particular type of use.

Political Considerations
Another thing you may want to consider is whether anything you are planning under your revised mission, is going to impact churches or charities in your local area (both inside and outside your denomination) or your neighbors. Sometimes this may be a facility location issue such as another nearby church has a food ministry and now you are starting a food ministry and the other church feels encroached upon. Other times it might be that you have decided to champion some social justice cause (immigration for example) and now you have anti-immigrant activists picketing outside your building. This is not to imply that you shouldn't do the right thing, this is just to remind you that if you are an organization in a structured accountability system, your superiors may not be happy to suddenly see your organization on the six o'clock news. And sometimes you just have to take into account the residential neighbors. When CMC became home to a prison ministry, the neighbors mounted a semi-organized protest because they didn't want (ex)prisoners coming into "their" neighborhood. They already were upset that CMC "attracted homeless people" into their neighborhood by giving away food and clothing. This is where your integrity comes into question and you have to do the right thing God laid upon you, whether it is the popular thing or not. But there are some public relations type things you can do to minimize these things. A big part of it is communications with those who would feel impacted, *before* these changes take place.

Choice School: A Safe Place
Just when I thought we are as crowded as physically possible, I was delighted and amazed at how God "squeezed in" yet another ministry at Christ Ministry Center. And it is not a small ministry, either. It is a high school! CMC became a site for Choice Community School, operated jointly by the San Diego County Office of Education and Juvenile Court.

How do you fit a dozen congregations, another dozen charities or weekday ministries, and a high school class into one building? (It reminds me of the old question, "How do you fit a dozen clowns into a VW? Easy! Six in the front seat and six in the back.")

In addition to the Sanctuary, Chapel and Social Hall, we have a "Lower Level" that offers additional space. As part of the 1957 educational wing expansion, this basement space was for many years the Youth Department of Christ Church. Recently it has served as additional worship space for Be Encouraged in the Word and our Hispanic ministry. Both of those congregations graciously moved to other spaces in our building to allow Choice School exclusive use of the Lower Level.

Choice Community School (CCS) is for students in grades 7 to 12. Rather than functioning as a traditional high school where all classes meet in one building, Choice School students meet in "self-contained" satellite classrooms spread throughout San Diego. In conjunction with Juvenile Court and Community Schools (JCCS), Choice School provides a fully-accredited educational program for school-age youth who are either wards of the court or have been referred by social services, probation, or one of the 42 school districts in San Diego County. Services are provided to incarcerated youth, pregnant minors, teen single mothers, foster youth, expelled teens, and chronically truant youth, students in drug treatment centers and group homes for neglected or abused children, and homeless youth.

JCCS serves about 12,000 students per year with 40 schools that are split between two networks that cover the entire county. JCCS educators are committed to high expectations, social justice, and equality for all students. They value diversity and strive to eradicate institutionalized racism and discrimination in all forms. Their priority is to raise achievement of all students while eliminating the achievement gap between students who are racially diverse. They accomplish this through the delivery of culturally and linguistically responsive standards-driven instruction, courageous and advocacy-oriented leadership, and relevant professional development. All JCCS community members stand personally committed and professionally accountable for the achievement of this mission.

Choice School fits perfectly with our mission to assist the hungry, thirsty, unclothed, sick, imprisoned, and sojourners among us. What an awesome opportunity to help 100 teenagers every weekday, year round, who are at a life-changing, life-defining crossroad, take the right path.

When the Juvenile Court and Community School began meeting in our basement, I wondered if they would feel it was an adequate and appropriate place for them to complete their high school education. My fears were set aside when the Principal said the comment she heard from the students over and over again was, *"We feel safe here."*

A Ministry Center is a place where the community can come and feel it is a good and safe place to find nourishment for body and soul.

This is God's doing. If you don't believe in miracles just look at the ongoing "Miracle on 33rd Street". A dozen clowns in a VW? That's a piece of cake. A dozen churches, another dozen charities and now a high school class all in one building? Now that's what I call a Miracle.

Chapter 17: What Legal Issues Do We Address?
(Assessing Regulations)

"This engraving—who does it look like? And whose name is on it?" They said, "Caesar." Then give Caesar what is his, and give God what is his." (Matthew 22:20-21)

The decision to transition from church to Ministry Center has many legal implications. We sought legal counsel to guide us through decisions with long lasting consequences. Each church is unique, so our circumstances may not match yours. The following is not legal advice, but simply an attempt to share some items you might consider.

New Corporation versus Amended Articles
The first decision we had to make was should we create a new corporation or more simply amend the Articles of Incorporation? In California, churches are usually already corporations under state law.

Our legal counsel advised us the Secretary of State is less likely to transfer assets from one non-profit to another. If we created a new corporation, we might not be able to transfer the assets (buildings, parsonages and other tangible assets) to the new corporation. While not impossible, we might incur considerable legal expenses and time to complete.

A simpler approach was to file an amendment to the existing Articles of Incorporation. This would involve not only a name change, but a re-statement of purpose for the corporation and a new set of By-Laws. (See Appendix E.) That includes a Conflict of Interest Policy each Director and Officer must sign. (See Appendix F.)

We elected to amend the Articles. (See Appendix G). In so doing, we learned the original corporation was formed in 1912 as First Church of the United Brethren in Christ of San Diego, Inc. That corporation underwent a second amendment in 1946 when it merged with the Evangelical Association and became First Evangelical United Brethren Church of San Diego, Inc. Once again, in 1970, after merger with The Methodist Church, the corporation was amended to become Christ United Methodist Church of San Diego, Inc. Since each of the prior amendments were for church name changes, all continuing to operate with consistent purposes, the first three amendments were relatively simply changes. However, the fourth amendment in 2012 involved not only a name change to Christ Ministry

Center, but a restatement of purpose. The corporation was no longer a church, but now was a Ministry Center.

The bottom line is either route you take, new corporation or amend the articles of the existing corporation, may be more involved than you estimate.

A Rose by Any Other Name
An initial task is deciding on a new name for your new organization, if you haven't already done so. The choices are endless. You may want to keep the same name. That certainly makes things easier because you don't have to change the name of your corporation/entity with the Secretary of State; or the IRS, or the myriad of other places where your legal name is, or change your physical signage. However, the drawback of keeping the same name doesn't convey the radical transition you are making to the rest of the world. Keeping your old name visibly ties you to the old purpose, and evokes memories in people's minds that things are "business as usual" for your organization. If possible, you may want to choose a name that conveys in one or two words what your new purpose is. It is free and permanent advertising.

Decide whether the word "church" will appear in the new name. That is understandable because what a church is and should be doing is consistent with your new purpose. The drawback is that having "church" in your name conveys mostly "just" religious services to the world. There is nothing wrong with that, but again, it doesn't announce your expanded purpose.

Decide whether your denomination affiliation will be in the new name. (Maybe you have been told that you must put your denomination affiliation in the new name.) There are pros and cons to that as well. Having a very prominent denomination in your name does imply stability and religious connections which are good things. One concern in doing that is we live in an increasingly digital society. After you decide on a name and add in your denomination, it could be quite lengthy and not what you want to have to type in for a website or in texting, or even in talking. No one ever wants to say "Go down to Holy Angels Blessing Our Lives in Times of Trouble Brethren Free Evangelical Ministry Center and see if they can help you."

In San Diego, we went from "Christ United Methodist Church" to (legally) "Christ United Methodist Ministry Center". However, after a few years it became apparent that it was such a mouthful, we informally adopted

110

"Christ Ministry Center" because it was easier to hone down to "CMC" (vice "CUMMC"). But as far as the Secretary of State and the IRS are concerned, we are still "Christ United Methodist Ministry Center". This was in no way an attempt to distance ourselves from The United Methodist Church.

One of the things you might also consider at this point is if there is a website domain name available for the name you want (or some abbreviation thereof). I am assisting a church in becoming a Ministry Center, and they have chosen for their new name "Faith on 54th" *(because they are on 54th Street)*. That is short, catchy and rolls off the tongue, their location is contained in the name, and they could get a domain name for it.

The name you choose for your organization is important because it is the first impression people get of your organization. As Indiana Jones was told: *"Choose wisely."* (*You will probably need a logo and a slogan too, but that can come later.*)

Members or Not

A critical issue is whether your new (or amended) corporation will be a member or non-member corporation. As a church, the members of the corporation are the members of the church. However, since Christ Ministry Center no longer operated as a church, there were no "members" in the classical sense. So we opted to be a "non-member" corporation, governed by a Board of Directors (Trustees).

Here is a word of caution for small congregations. If you have, for instance, a dozen members left in your legacy congregation and are the owners or operators of a million dollar building, what happens if suddenly 13 new members join the church and form a new majority? That opens the possibility that the legacy congregation could be the victim of a "hostile takeover" in business terms.

Non-profit and 501(c)(3)

Another major consideration was whether we would, as a legal United Methodist entity, use the blanket Internal Revenue Service 501(c)(3) declaration shared by all UMC churches and agencies, or seek our own unique 501(c)(3) declaration. Almost always when a new church applies for an Employee Identification Number (EIN), necessary to open a bank account or issue payroll, the IRS states that, as a church or religious organization, they grant (at least temporarily) 501(c)(3) status. That does not mean you have a unique 501(c)(3) identity. Plus, there is a technical distinction between being a non-profit and being a 501(c)(3). Consult your attorney for the applicable laws that enable your donors to receive tax deductible credit for contributions.

We opted to seek our own 501(c)(3). The reason was that we may in the future want to apply for grants. More and more grant applications require an individual 501(c)(3) number.

Filing for your own 501(c)(3) identity is an involved and painstaking process. Be prepared to wait up to a year or more for the IRS to issue a ruling.

The IRS Form 1023, see Appendix H, is an extensive document requiring considerable reflection and research. As painful as it was to complete, in hindsight it was one of the most helpful tools in defining Christ Ministry Center.

Function: Direct Help or Helping the Helpers
IMPORTANT: The IRS Form 1023 wanted to know if we were providing help directly to individuals (such as food, clothing, shelter, etc.) Or, were we providing help to organizations who provide help directly to individuals. Of course we wanted to say we help directly, but it was an eye-opener to realize our role was to help the helpers, who in turn provide direct help to individuals.

Your church may become a Ministry Center that provides direct help, or like CMC, provides help to the helpers. This is a critical distinction.

So how are you going to function? Specifically, are you envisioning providing charitable services *directly* to clientele, or are you intending to provide those services *through a renter and/or partner*? When completing IRS Form 1023, *Application for Recognition of Exemption under Section 501(c)(3) of the IRS Code* (this is to get your organization's tax exempt status and number); you will be required to identify the type of '*public charitable status*' you are claiming as the basis for your exemption.

(Excerpt from the IRS Form 1023) "Organizations that are exempt under sections 501(c)(3) are private foundations unless they are:
- *churches, schools, or hospitals...*
- *organizations that support one or more other organization(s) that are themselves classified as public charities"*

You may be thinking, "we'll just check the box that says 'church' on that form because we have 'church' in our name, and we have been a church since creation, and because we are going to have the 'legacy congregation' continue to worship here". I'm certainly not qualified to offer legal/tax advice, but even the IRS says they "do not have a single definition for 'church' for tax purposes" and so they will apply some common characteristics of churches to what you are doing and then decide if you're a church or not.

Christ Ministry Center San Diego for example, is an *"organization that supports one or more other organization(s) that are themselves classified as public charities"* under the IRS Codes. This type of organization does not *directly* provide ministries that offer food, clothes, and so forth; but provides building spaces, and other benefits to the charities and churches which do.

Just as Christ Ministry Center chose to be an organization that "supports other 501(c)(3) organizations" and is not, in the classical sense, a "church"; that enabled us to separate our legacy congregation from the Ministry Center. That was a huge decision because of the consequences. That one decision not only drove our new IRS tax exemption status but also:

- Transferred responsibility for that church's income and expenses (such as salaries for worship leaders and musical directors) to them.
- Took the debt on the building off of their shoulders.
- Relieved the United Methodist denomination from having to provide a minister for them.
- Allowed them to operate fairly autonomously to grow or close.
- Allowed them to be exempt from the financial burden of the Methodist's apportionment system.
- Relieved the new Ministry Center from having to operate both the Ministry Center and a church.
- Formed the basis for the Ministry Center to collect rent from that church.

But even more importantly (when being visionary), Christ Church had been slowly dying for decades. When closure was to inevitably happen, where would that leave the new Ministry Center? Both Ministry Center and church would be lost.

Business Considerations

It is time to put your 'business person' hat on over your religious hat. Consider what the differences this one decision makes: Providing services directly would likely entail hiring a large staff (paying their salaries), providing rent free spaces, and funding their supplies. The result of that method is all cost to the new organization and no income. Providing caring ministries to the community from your location through renting and/or partnering with existing charitable organizations, allows those same ministries to be performed from your spaces, but without the expense or hassle involved, and you derive an income stream (rent) so these ministries can continue to happen.

This is not to persuade or dissuade you from choosing one operational model (and charitable status) or the other. This is just something that has serious ramifications to be considered.

Form 990 (Return of Organization - Exempt From Income Tax)

Although the IRS said we were exempt from filing the full Form 990 rather than the postcard Form 990-EZ, we opted for the requirement to file the full form each year. That was to insure full transparency in our finances. Form 990 must be filed by May 15 of each year.

Deeds and Trust Clause

Once the Secretary of State approved the amended Articles, it was necessary to make sure the deeds for our buildings and two parsonages were properly updated. This took a bit more effort than planned because we discovered one deed for a parsonage was never updated when the first amendment took place in 1946. It was a bit surreal for me to convene a meeting of the Trustees of a corporation formed in 1912 and technically ceased to exist in 1946, before I was born. Yet, as President of the legal successor corporation, I signed documents that informed the County of our new name.

As United Methodists, while the local congregation does not own the buildings and parsonages, we must hold them "in trust" for the denomination. In simple terms, we cannot sell or encumber the property, but we are the Trustees charged with the maintenance and operation of the property. The Ministry Center's statement of purpose in the amended Articles, By-Laws and Deeds of Trust must all agree using the current legal criteria. Arriving at language that the County, Secretary of State, State Board of Equalization and IRS all agreed upon took several iterations.

Once again, prepare yourself for surprises and a learning curve. The older your church is, the more time you are likely to spend going through dusty old records, either at your church or the courthouse.

Property Tax Changes
As a legal non-profit, your building may qualify for tax exemptions. However, please be aware that anyone who uses your building must also be tax exempt or you may lose your exemption, or portion used by that organization.

The process in California is complex. First, anyone using our facilities more than one day a week must obtain an Organization Clearance Certificate (OCC) from the State Board of Equalization. Once obtained, the organization does not need to reapply for the OCC, unless the organization legally reorganizes.

Then, no later than February 15 of each year, the organization using space in the Ministry Center, must file a Welfare Exemption Form with the County Tax Assessor. The County will verify an OCC is in effect, and will grant tax exemption for that organization for that year. But be aware that if you have four organizations using your sanctuary for example; even if three have their OCC, but one does not, you are liable for taxes on 100% of the sanctuary – not 25%.

IMPORTANT: Failing to obtain an OCC and failing to annually file the Welfare Tax Exemption Form in a timely manner will subject your property to losing its tax exemption. You will then receive a tax bill that could otherwise be avoided.

Certainly not all states have a property tax system like California, but a number of them have similar systems. Check with your attorney or tax accountant regarding the applicable laws and regulations in your state.

Board of Directors
Whether you organize as a member or non-member corporation, you must have a governing Board. As a United Methodist entity, we followed the Book of Discipline's guidelines, which included (1) suggested no less than three and no more than nine members, (2) the majority of Directors shall be United Methodists, and (3) inclusion of ethnic and gender diversity.

We selected nine Directors and divided them into three "classes" so that three rotate off each year, and a new class is elected each year. The class that rotates off is eligible to be reelected for another three-year term, but may serve no more than six consecutive years.

Also, the Board should reflect the mission of the Ministry Center. Our unstated goal is for CMC to become "the place" in our community where people come to find food, clothing, shelter, counseling, and dozens of other types of help. Therefore, we included as Directors members from the greater community.

Lease Contract

Do you have existing contracts? What are they for (rentals or services)? Do any need to be terminated or extended? If you are moving to a predominantly landlord status, do you have adequate contract templates?

We have a contract for each organization that uses our building. It is for one year, and should be renewed annually, or else it goes onto a month-to-month basis. We found that giving the Ministry Center and the organization a 60-day "escape clause" was best. If things go badly, it is usually more damaging to hold someone to the end of the contract. At least that is what we have experienced.

Our contract requires:
- At least one-million-dollar liability insurance naming CMC as beneficiary.
- Organization must be non-profit
- Organization must have obtained (or actively applied for) Organizational Clearance Certificate with the State Board of Equalization
- Signed acceptance of our Building Use Policy

An example of our Lease Contract appears in Appendix I. However, you should obtain legal counsel in forming your contracts.

Building Use Policy

Do you have a "building use policy" to mitigate liability? An example of our Building Use Policy appears in Appendix J.

Building Compliance and Zoning Codes

There are a myriad of zoning and compliance matters to consider. Among the ones we have dealt with are:
- Noise compliance and abatement
- Rainwater runoff into city drainage

- Trip and fall hazards
- Fire inspections
- Evacuation compliance

Chapter 18: Are Our "Faithful Few" Enough?
(Assessing Spiritual Will)

"I see what you've done. Now see what I've done. I've opened a door before you that no one can slam shut. You don't have much strength; I know that; you used what you had to keep my Word. You didn't deny me when times were rough. Because you kept my Word in passionate patience, I'll keep you safe in the time of testing." (Revelations 3:8,10)

In this chapter, this assessment will help you determine if you and your congregation have faith that, with God's help, you can succeed as a Ministry Center. We look at both the faith to make the bold changes, and the role of the legacy congregation members in the new structure.

Can We Make It?
In Luke 17:6, Jesus said, *"You don't need more faith. There is no 'more' or 'less' in faith. If you have a bare kernel of faith, say the size of a poppy seed, you could say to this sycamore tree, 'Go jump in the lake,' and it would do it." (The Message)*

The following may be helpful and inspirational to know you need not "go it alone".

Are You Spiritually Prepared?
"Anointing" is one of those terms in the Bible right alongside sanctified and justified that sounds a bit mystical to the average reader. In reality, anointing simply means you are called for a purpose, divinely prepared and blessed to succeed. Here are some illustrations of how God anointed Christ Ministry Center using the story of Moses as a reference.

(1) Called for a Purpose
First, anointing (in this context) means being called for a purpose. None of us doubt God had a plan for Moses from his conception and birth. But God has a plan and purpose for every life. *"I knew you before I formed you in your mother's womb. Before you were born I set you apart and appointed you as my prophet to the nations." (Jeremiah 1:5).*

This is no less true for churches. Every church and congregation began with a vision, a mission, and a purpose.

(2) Divinely Prepared

Second, this anointing comes with divine preparations. God gives each of us unique gifts and talents to accomplish our purpose. God will never ask us to do something we are not equipped (blessed) to do. And the same holds true for your church!

Look at how God prepared Moses for that divine purpose of leading the children of Israel from Captivity to the Promised Land.

- The first 40 years of Moses' life was spent in Pharaoh's house. From his miraculous rescue afloat in a basket by Pharaoh's daughter, to his real mother being chosen as his nurse, to Moses becoming an "adopted son" of Pharaoh, God was teaching Moses the inner workings of Egyptian government – an invaluable resource he would later need when he demanded, "Let my people go!".
- The second 40 years, Moses learned to survive in the back side of the desert. After slaying an Egyptian for striking a Hebrew, Moses fled to the desert. No doubt, he felt his life was over. But God was giving him the second blessing he would need to accomplish his ultimate purpose: how to lead thousands of people through the desert.
- At age 80, when most folks think their life stories are complete, God used Moses to do what his purpose was from the beginning. Moses was uniquely qualified to lead the exodus. Only Moses knew the inner workings of the Egyptian government and how to survive in the wilderness. This was no coincidence.

(3) Blessed to Succeed

Third, God supplies our every need (not every want, but every need) from God's riches in glory. (Philippians 4:19). It doesn't mean escape from problems and conflict. But it means when we need a sea parted, God has our backs. We may not dine on sumptuous meals, but manna is always there every morning.

Moses was anointed. That means he was called for a purpose, equipped for the task, and blessed along the way at precisely God's perfect timing.

Anointing in this context is divine, but not so mysterious as to be misunderstood. Moses was not perfect. Neither are any of us. He died within eyesight of the Promised Land, full of years at age 120. His life was a journey of anointing and blessings that enabled God's people to arrive at their destination.

Anointing = called for a purpose + equipped for service + blessed to succeed

If God's plan for your struggling church is to become a Ministry Center, God will show you the vision, divinely prepare you (maybe you have been and are being prepared already), and supply the blessings you need at just the right time.

The more I look back, the more I am convinced that I, too, was "anointed" (called, prepared, blessed) to lead Christ Church through the uncharted wilderness to become Christ Ministry Center. "Lest any man should boast," this is all God's doing.

The Role of Legacy Congregation and Members
Sometimes the "faithful few" may be not be the best leaders for the new Ministry Center. The next chapter deals with the leaders needed and the qualities of leadership those leaders should possess.

There is a reason the "faithful few" are few in number. Often that is because they have not been able to make the adjustments needed to turn the tide of decline. But there is a definite role for the legacy members under certain circumstances.

When Christ Church became Christ Ministry Center, we agreed that the legacy congregation would continue to worship, but not as a chartered United Methodist congregation. This was a liberating distinction for them. No longer were they responsible for the upkeep of an aging building, of providing a full pastor's salary and benefits package, or contributing to United Methodists' apportionments (fair-share of denominational expenses).

The legacy congregation had declined to about two dozen members. Fortunately, a lay minister who was a lifelong member of Christ Church was available to provide lay pastoral leadership. The legacy congregation chose to call themselves Christ Chapel. Though small in number, their reduced burden of expenses enabled them to operate "in the black" from day one.

In Chapter 28 there is the story of a new congregation that arose from the closure of Christ Church. Christ Chapel is now part of the new Exodus

United Methodist Church. It is, as our Bishop stated, *"a Resurrection story"*.

Respect for Church Legacy
It is most natural that the legacy members may feel they are being cast aside. It requires diplomacy and grace to navigate this matter. Of course, the old church may have been destined to close with the absolute casting aside that goes with closure. In leading a church to become a Ministry Center, it is important to treat the heritage of the former congregation with respect. In so doing you will provide a pathway for their continued role in vital ministry.

Entering the Promised Land
After centuries in Egyptian exile in, and after 40 years of wandering in the wilderness, the Israelites finally came to the banks of the Jordan River, the last obstacle to possessing the Promised Land. What impresses me most about Joshua 3: 7-17 is how anti-climactic it was. The promise, given to Abraham, was finally about to be realized.

The same struggle between faith and fear they had experienced in Egypt and in the wilderness confronted the Hebrews as they stood on the banks of the promise's fulfillment. First, the river was at flood stage. Who wants to cross a flooded river without a bridge, or a boat? Yet, when by faith they stepped into the river, the river parted, just as the Red Sea had done years before, and they were able to cross on dry ground.

It takes faith to step into the stormy river. But unless we exercise that kind of faith, we will never enter the Promised Land.

There is a big difference in casting a wistful eye into the Promised Land and in possessing it! It takes simple, yet determined steps of faith to possess the promises of God.

"I am bound for the Promised Land,
I am bound for the Promised Land.
Oh, who will come and go with me,
I am bound for the Promised Land."

Chapter 19: What Leadership Do We Need?
(Assessing Human Resources)

"I have a special concern for you church leaders. I know what it's like to be a leader, in on Christ's sufferings as well as the coming glory. Here's my concern: that you care for God's flock with all the diligence of a shepherd. Not because you have to, but because you want to please God. Not calculating what you can get out of it, but acting spontaneously. Not bossily telling others what to do, but tenderly showing them the way." (1 Peter 5:1-3)

This chapter looks at the leaders and leadership skills necessary to succeed as a Ministry Center. First, we should define what we mean by leadership.

Warren Bennis, widely regarded as a pioneer of the contemporary field of leadership studies, defines it this way: "Leadership is the capacity to translate vision into reality."

From Where Do Leaders Come?
In Ephesians, we learn that God provides leaders. *"He handed out gifts of apostle, prophet, evangelist, and pastor-teacher to train Christ's followers in skilled servant work, working within Christ's body, the church, until we're all moving rhythmically and easily with each other, efficient and graceful in response to God's Son, fully mature adults, fully developed within and without, fully alive like Christ." (Ephesians 4:12-13)*

Notice that there are a variety of roles. With the proper mix of leaders and gifts, things operate rhythmically and efficiently.

What are the Needed Leadership Positions in a Ministry Center?
When my District Superintendent asked for advice on my replacement, I told him it might be more important that my successor have a Master of Business Administration (MBA) degree than a Master of Divinity (M.Div.) degree. Ideally, he or she should have both.

The leader of a Ministry Center should have (1) good business knowledge, (2) an entrepreneurial spirit, (3) a strong faith, and (4) an understanding of urban ministry with an ecumenical spirit.

After reading my job description, one of my Board members said a person who meets all the requirements and fulfills all the functions described in it should be paid "at least six figures". (Suffice it to say, I am not being paid six figures.) No doubt finding the right leader with the right gifts and graces will not be easy. But I am convinced God provides the right leaders for each situation. And thank God, salary and benefits are not the driving forces motivating these leaders. Appendix K offers a job description for the director of CMC.

Christ Ministry Center has three staff members: Director, Office Manager, and Church Sexton. We are fortunate to have two parsonages located adjacent to the building. The Office Manager lives in one parsonage. Our Sexton, the person who opens and closes the building daily and is the first line of defense when emergencies (such as broken pipes) arise, lives in the other. Having these two staff living on-site is a blessing to the Ministry Center, and also serves as part of their compensation.

So operating a Ministry Center does not require a large staff, depending upon available resources and the extent of the work being done.

We hire a custodial service to clean the building rather than hire one directly, mostly because of the premium required for worker's compensation. A custodian is more likely to suffer injury on the job than an office worker, and worker's compensation insurance is pricey.

What are the Qualities of Ministry Center Leaders?
Titus 1:7-9 says, *"It's important that a church leader, responsible for the affairs in God's house, be looked up to—not pushy, not short-tempered, not a drunk, not a bully, not money-hungry. He or she must welcome people, be helpful, wise, fair, and reverent, have a good grip on themselves, and have a good grip on the Message, knowing how to use the truth to either spur people on in knowledge or stop them in their tracks if they oppose it."*

Below are the top ten character traits for leaders, according to multiple surveys.
- Fair
- Humble
- Wise (i.e., Vision)
- Courageous
- Honest
- Trustworthy
- Self-disciplined
- Committed
- Optimistic
- Compassionate

Community of Innovation

Dr. Lovett Weems is Director of the Lewis Center for Leadership at Wesley Theological Seminary in Washington, D.C. The Lewis Center offers insightful and timely articles on the role of church leaders in our changing world.

In a recent article, Dr. Weems wrote: *"One leader, even one with a compelling vision, is insufficient for spirit-led innovative leadership. The innovative leader must create a community of innovation by developing both an atmosphere and the people capable of functioning in a more complex and chaotic environment."*

A Ministry Center is a "community of innovation" with an atmosphere where people may function, offering their own gifts and graces, in a complex and often chaotic (ever-changing) environment.

Leader and Manager in Implementation and Ongoing Management Phases

Leadership and management require different skills. The leadership needed to transition from church to Ministry Center may not be the same needed to manage the Ministry Center once it is established.

"Esprit de Corp" Starts at the Top

I would like to tell you that every church or charity that comes into partnership with you will have the same level of devotion and respect for your Ministry Center as you. Unfortunately, that is not true.

We found that some, like Exodus Church, from the very first day have been committed to leaving the building in better shape than they found it. Others have proved the old adage *"No one changes the oil in a rented car!"*

The attitude starts at the top, with the pastor. Leaders set the tone for everything that happens within their church or charity. And that holds true for the Ministry Center's leaders as well.

SECTION FOUR: Ministry Center Implementation & Management

Chapter 20: How Do We Make "The Decision"?
(Discerning)

"So here's what I think: The best thing you can do right now is to finish what you started last year and not let those good intentions grow stale. Your heart's been in the right place all along. You've got what it takes to finish it up, so go to it. Once the commitment is clear, you do what you can, not what you can't. The heart regulates the hands. This isn't so others can take it easy while you sweat it out. No, you are shoulder to shoulder with them all the way, your surplus matching their deficit, their surplus matching your deficit. In the end you come out even." (2 Corinthians 8:10-14)

Once you make assessments, you decide the main decision: is this for us?

Weighing the Pros and Cons

Are There Any "Showstoppers"?
Showstoppers are any circumstances that are insurmountable, maybe a total lack of financial support; project disapproved/stonewalled at a higher level; buildings needing extensive/expensive repairs (more than $250K); state or county laws that prohibit you from proceeding; liens filed against the property; injunctions filed against your plan proceeding; etc. It is impossible to even imagine all the things that could derail you. In California I have seen such things as a "Least Tern" or "snail darter" halt multimillion water projects that would have alleviated some of the severe Southern California drought. Suffice it to say if you uncover any information possibly detrimental to your plan, investigate it thoroughly.

Can You Mitigate the Weaknesses and Leverage the Strengths?
Sometimes it helps to look at the strengths and weaknesses of what you have (the facilities, assets, finances, personnel, etc.) in conjunction with what you want to do. You want to mitigate the weaknesses and leverage the strengths. For example, if there is a great deal of debt on the building (weakness) is there anything you can brainstorm that might be able to diminish that?

There is always going to be something that makes what you want to do difficult. Learn the difference between difficult and impossible. Can you find "workarounds" or solutions to the difficult items? Can you alter your plans slightly to avoid a hard spot?

CMC had a number of "weaknesses" when we started: lack of funds, plenty of debt, poor condition of the building, the reluctance and even opposition from the current congregation, an initial lack of a clear vision and plan, the difficulty of creating something that was not covered in the Methodist discipline, and much more. There were also a number of weaknesses/problems that were not even known initially, but reared their ugly heads in the implementation process. I can only classify them in one category: my ignorance of both the process and ramifications of such things as the necessity to locate, obtain, decipher, and sort through deeds and mergers of what turned out to be a 100+ year old corporation *(the former/existing church);* the complex and overlapping San Diego County tax laws; the difficulty in understanding and complying with the requirements of establishing a corporation in California; the length of time to obtain a 501(c)(3) (non-profit) tax status, and on and on.

Likewise, you want to leverage or maximize your strengths. These might be tangible (such as a sizeable bank account), or intangible like people involved who will help you succeed through their large network of contacts; or people who may enthusiastically serve on your team with skills, knowledge or experience vital to necessary tasks. Or even the goodwill your church may have in the community.

CMC had a number of strengths when they started: a very large building, a decent sized parking lot, an excellent location, support from their denomination superiors, people with the skills to make it work, but mostly continuous help from God.

Three Critical "Must Haves"

ABC3 of Success
There are really only three pieces you must have to succeed:

1. **Attitude.** The right attitude is necessary for converting to a Ministry Center or running a Ministry Center. The sections of this book have explained how your heart, mind, and spirit have to be aligned and attuned to God and the needs of the people you are helping. You have to know in your soul that God is with you and will ensure your success.

2. **Business Plan.** Your business plan has to support a Ministry Center model, either the one we followed or one of your own. If you don't have the right business plan, it is unlikely that you can sustain the Ministry Center long term. Appendix B shows a successful Business Plan. This is not the only plan, but whatever plan you adopt has to provide enough revenue to be self-supporting initially and for the foreseeable future.

3. **Capacity, Configuration, and Condition** of your building. If your building doesn't support your Ministry Center model, it is almost impossible to succeed. Using your building to generate revenue to support the good works of a Ministry Center is critical to success – unless you have a totally different revenue stream in mind.

All three of these are necessary for success. If you have all three, then your odds of being successful increase dramatically. However, if you are lacking any of the three above, the odds of being successful decrease substantially.

What Is the Likelihood of Success?
One of the greatest predictors of success in revitalizing your organization is not included in your black or white assessments. It lies in the personnel involved and how much faith, strength, enthusiasm, and vision they have for the task. God can make anything happen. Your key people on the team and their superiors above them have to believe this is the right thing and it *can* work, and that with God's help, it *will* work. Anyone chosen to be involved in this transition has to have that absolute belief.

People may say that I "caught lightning in a bottle" in creating the Ministry Center in San Diego. I prefer to think that I "caught grace in a bottle" because of all the unmerited blessings the Lord gave me in this endeavor. I was blissfully ignorant as to what it would take to create a Ministry Center.

Heck, I didn't even know what a Ministry Center was and now I run one!

When I started the process of creating CMC (which I didn't even recognize as a process), I was just following the directive God laid on my heart: feed the hungry, clothe the naked; help the sick, strangers and imprisoned......
God sent me all the people I needed to succeed, and all the opportunities, funding, and wisdom I needed. As puzzle pieces kept miraculously falling into place, my vision and understanding became greater and greater. Our multitude of blessings increasingly became referred to in our inner circle as

"a God thing" because no human alone could have made things happen the way they did. I continue to be amazed, honored and humbled that God chose me for this.

Now people come to me and want to know in ten words or less how they can save their church from closing. I never saw it that way in my experience. I did see that my congregation was graying and dwindling. I prayed long and hard as to why this was happening and what God wanted me to do about it. I had a fear that there could be a "For Sale" sign on our church lawn one day. But God didn't lose faith in me, and kept impressing on my heart that it wasn't those few hours on Sunday morning that I was to be concerned about. It was the 24 hours a day that His children needed someone to tend them in their travails. My fear dissipated when I became more and more concerned about caring for all of God's children, and less and less concerned about the number of people in the Sanctuary for one hour on Sunday, or the amount in the offering plate. The scales had fallen from my eyes. *"I once was blind and now I see."*

What Do I Do Now to Get Approvals?
Some denominations have an established chain of authority (e.g. Methodists, Lutherans, Catholics, etc.); and some churches are independent and may or may not have another entity who has approval authority for changing directions. Unless you are a totally independent church, before you can seriously start an assessment of making radical changes, you have to know who would need to be on board with any changes contemplated, and be prepared (if this is your idea) to sway them to your side. Probably the best way to do this is to bring up the topic theoretically with your immediate supervisor, and see if he/she would even entertain the notion. If you and your supervisor (district superintendent, bishop, monsignor, etc.) want to float this concept any higher, you are going to have to have a fairly well developed concept and assessment of how this would/could work. Also, you are going to have to have knowledge of any denominational policies that may apply; how much it could cost; where the money would be coming from; and how it impacts any other churches in your denomination and area. You are going to have to consider how this change could be better for not only your church, but beneficial for your district, state, conference, etc. and have tangible, concrete reasons or facts to prove it. By reading this book, you should be better prepared to make such a presentation to your superiors.

He Who Hesitates is Lost

Many churches only begin to consider the notion of becoming a Ministry Center when they have been informed that a decision has already been made from above to close their church. It is pretty near impossible to change the direction of that bullet when it has already left the gun. By then, money decisions have usually been made (such as selling the building) and where the money would go, future personnel changes have been programmed and major adjustments have already occurred or are in process. There are always exceptions, but a good leader should have seen that eventuality coming and started the process of seeking alternatives long before they get that death sentence.

Knowledge and Wisdom

You obtain knowledge through the assessments where you gather facts and figures. Wisdom is the application of that knowledge in making the decision to become a Ministry Center, or not.

Here are some guidelines to help as you seek wisdom in making this crucial decision.

1. Wisdom is a gift. Knowledge is acquired. If you must work for something, it is not a gift, it is wages. God still invites us to seek, ask and find wisdom, as Solomon did.
2. Wisdom springs from the spirit. Knowledge springs from the mind. There is a spiritual dimension to wisdom that science excludes. If you cannot see it, measure it, or test it, science says it does not exist.
3. Wisdom increases over time. Knowledge diminishes with age. Medical doctors, lawyers, and other professions must continually work to keep their knowledge current. While the body of knowledge grows, our mind's capacity to remember diminishes with age. Wisdom increases so that the oldest in society are often seen as the wisest.
4. Wisdom matures with experience. Knowledge matures with learning. A wise person will continue to make wise decisions throughout life, while knowledge is a life-long, ever-growing struggle to keep current. Wisdom helps keep emotions and passions in check.
5. Wisdom focuses on understanding. Knowledge focuses on facts. Wisdom is making the practical and prudent application of knowledge.

6. Wisdom helps you make good choices and decisions. Knowledge helps in performing a skill or task. Or expressed another way, knowledge is a tool; wisdom is understanding how to use the tool. Wisdom helps focus on our long term goals, the future and consequences for actions.
7. Wisdom is common sense. Knowledge is education. Knowledge and education are good. But wisdom is better.

Making "the decision" will require a lot of prayer. Include in your prayers the request for wisdom to discern and do God's will.

Chapter 21: What Are the Strategic Decisions?
(Planning)

"A soldier on duty doesn't get caught up in making deals at the marketplace. He concentrates on carrying out orders. An athlete who refuses to play by the rules will never get anywhere. It's the diligent farmer who gets the produce. Think it over. God will make it all plain." (2 Timothy 2:5-7)

I had the unique opportunity to work with the best technical and strategic minds for over a decade as technology operations manager at a large San Diego water utility. What I learned from these visionaries is that organizational survival depends upon the strategic vision of the leaders, and the corresponding support of members in achieving the vision. Or, as the Bible puts it: *"Where there is no vision, the people perish."*

Realizing many clergy have no such opportunity, I feel a responsibility accompanies this privilege. What I learn about strategic technology management, I attempt to apply to the church. While the church is not a "business," that fact does not excuse the church from responsible strategic planning. Jesus was a strategic visionary who practiced (and expects from us) good church management and stewardship.

Like most institutions, the church is slow to change, and often the last to implement and benefit from technical and strategic best practices. I invite clergy and laity to share a vision of "The Strategic Church" to equip congregations in accomplishing their mission in this challenging and rapidly changing world.

It is essential that a church has a vision, and uses strategic decision-making in moving from the "as is" church to the "to be" church.

Plan Your Work Before You Work Your Plan
Now that "The Decision" has been made, and you have obtained any denominational or other approvals, don't jump on your horse and run off in all directions at once. There are still important decisions that have to be made before you can start implementation. The next step is to plan your work before starting to work your plan.

Strategic Decisions
Strategy is defined as *"a careful plan or method for achieving a particular goal usually over a long period of time"*. Strategic decisions deal with the

range of organizational activities. It is what the organization is to be like and to be about. Strategic decisions may involve major changes.

There are a number of strategic decisions to be made and below they've been grouped into the categories they relate to.

Category 1: Operational

Charities
Have you decided to rent space to charities? Are you going to have restrictions on the type of charities? This can be anything from whether or not they have 501(c)(3) designation; or the type of charitable work they are engaged in (such as a 12 step group for sexual addiction); or you just don't "feel" comfortable with their leader.

Churches
If you have decided to rent spaces to charities, are you also planning to rent spaces to other churches? Of various denominations? I can understand that not all current churches may welcome denominations foreign to their own. The downside (with your business hat on) is that a negative decision limits your pool of potential renters. For myself, I have always felt that the Bible doesn't distinguish between Catholics and Protestants in the Kingdom of God.

I am here to tell you, in a city the size of San Diego, there are dozens, if not hundreds, of small churches looking for worship space. We even have realtors exclusively specializing in finding homes for churches. It does my heart good to be able to welcome a small church to our building and be able to nurture and assist them in growing and getting established. We are happy when they grow too large for us and move on to bigger spaces. In this day, we need all the "churched" people we can manufacture. Many times when striking up a conversation with someone, I ask what church they belong to, and are continually surprised by how many say they are meeting in a school. I cannot help but think that confines them to one or two services on Sunday, and provides no office space, no storage space, no "social interaction" space, and no opportunity for mid-week Bible study. It is hard to grow a church that is so tightly constrained. We have a good sized (but not huge) Sanctuary (seating a few hundred), and a small Chapel (seating about 40). Currently we have one service after another in both the Sanctuary and Chapel on Sundays and if we had two or three more Chapels, we could fill them all. Our Seventh Day Adventist friends have the building mostly to themselves on Saturday for their very large group.

Currently all our "church renters" are Christian and Orthodox, but we do not limit ourselves to that. We would welcome other faiths the same as we would provide charity space to an organization such as Jewish Family Services.

Business Renters

Have you decided to rent to non-Christian/non-Church organizations, perhaps for the income needed? If so, are you going to have any restrictions on the type of business renters? As stated previously, be aware that renters who are not 501(c)(3) organizations may cause the portion of your building they use to become taxable under property tax laws.

Legacy Congregation

We have discussed the legacy congregation in several previous chapters. Now you have to make the conscious decision on what is going to become of them. Once that decision is made, then prepare to meet with them and inform them of the decision, what is going to become of them, and most importantly, when.

Staffing

Based on the previous decisions you made above, determine your future staffing. Future positions may include Director, Treasurer/bookkeeper, Administrative Assistant, Facility Manager; Contract Specialist; Custodial; Security; etc.; and write position descriptions for each. Appendix K is a Director's job description from CMC, as a jumping off point. Not all positons have to be paid and/or full time. Some may be volunteers; some could be part time. Salaries for new positions will also have to be determined based on your position descriptions.

Some positons could be filled through service contracts, such as the janitorial, bookkeeper, or even facility management. A word to the wise about having personnel work directly for you versus obtaining those services through a business or independent contractor. The advantage of having an employee work for you is that you can daily direct their schedules, and work assignments, and you feel that they are more trustworthy. The biggest disadvantages are that you have to manage their taxes, leave, health insurance, etc.; and pay their Workman's Compensation coverage which is expensive. The advantages of having a business provide the services are that you don't have to worry about coverage for their vacations or sicknesses (that's their business' issue); and you don't have to pay their FICA (social security and Medicare), or Workman's Compensation. Also their company should have liability and other insurance coverages which don't leave you holding the bag if something happens.

Current Staff
Besides just determining your future position needs, you have to decide what becomes of the current staff. Can they transition to your new positions or even do you want them to?

CMC in San Diego has a remarkably small staff, only the Director and the Office Manager are paid staff positons. The janitorial is done through a contract, and the payroll is handled by a payroll company. Security is provided through surveillance cameras. I am also an IT specialist and take care of the website, computers, network, servers, projectors, and Wi-Fi in the building. We have been very fortunate that my wife (retired after 45 years in the Federal Government), is a professional in a number of fields including contract management, financial management, facility management, repair, and process improvement, just to name a few; and she fills in many places where we are lacking. Best of all, she works for free!

Tenants
Much like your current staff, you have to take a look at any current tenants and determine if you want them to continue and if so, do you want to make adjustments in their spaces/rents.

Refine New Mission Statement
You should have by this point, at least initially concocted some type of mission/purpose statement. Now is the time to refine and polish it. Again, a mission statement is short and defines what an organization is, and why it exists, which is its reason for being. At a minimum, your mission statement should identify who your primary "clientele" are (who you are going to serve), and identify the services you will provide, at least in a generalized way. (You don't want to be really specific in naming the services you will provide because that could become a very fluid and changing thing as your organization evolves. You probably want to say something like "assisting the poor, distressed, and underprivileged" rather than "providing food and clothes to the poor…" and locking yourself into a narrow service and clientele area.)

The mission statement will be used in any documents you file such as with the Secretary of State or the IRS.

As a reminder, Christ Ministry Center's mission statement reads:

136

"The purpose of Christ United Methodist Ministry Center is to:
Provide a nurturing environment for worship, religious education and
fellowship for religious congregations in the advancement of religion and
ministry;
Provide a base of operations for charitable and community non-profit
organizations engaged in public benefit ministries; especially relief of the
poor, distressed and underprivileged;

Create and maintain a mechanism to harness the resources of existing
non-profit charities and churches in the San Diego area which enables
them more efficiency and effectiveness in helping the helpless."

Category 2: Financial

Show Me the Money
Some of the significant strategic questions are financial.
- Where is the money coming from during and after the transition?
- What is your financial model going to be when completed?
- What is the transition going to cost?

You can rightfully assume there will be costs for the transition even if it is
only "refreshing" the spaces. What money is going to be used for transition
and/or operational costs during transition? For example, are you going to
raise money specifically for the transition? How? If you have different
'buckets' of money available (offerings, rents, investments, savings/money
markets; capital improvements; and so forth), do you need to prioritize or
earmark them for transition money? If you use all the money you have
available for the transition/implementation and still need more, do you
have a plan for how/where to get additional funding? All of these are
decisions to be made as part of your financial strategy.

How will the new organization handle any current debt? (mortgages,
HELOC-line of credit, loans, etc.)

Are you going to use the same bank accounts you have now? Do you need
to open new ones, or do you need to add or delete current authorized
signers?

Category 3: Facilities

Identify the size of the elephant. I recommend you hire a professional
building inspector to go through all your church property (church building,

parsonages, other buildings, parking lot, etc.) and give you a formal report on what problems there are, an assessment of the severity of the problem *(minor, significant, major)*, and an approximate of what each would cost to repair. It is only then can you begin to make decisions on any actions you are going to take.

Categorizing the documented problems by legal, severity of usage impact, and risk may be a good start.

Legal facility problems are going to be items such as Americans with Disabilities Act (ADA) access, or failure to meet building codes. This is a calculated risk. It generally does not stop you from using these rooms/areas, but could increase your risk of a lawsuit or an injury.

Severity is going to be prioritizing as far as building usage, such as the Sanctuary has a severe roof leak and it makes it impossible to use when it rains; while the a/c not working does not really prohibit building usage.

Risk is going to be several things: (1) risk to the building, (2) risk to people, and (3) risk to other's property. Risk to the building may be something like the stained glass windows are going to fall out if something isn't done immediately to secure them, or there is a minor leak but left unrepaired will eventually cause major building damage and mold. Risk to people may be that the Sanctuary (or other) ceilings have damage and may fall and injure someone; or the sidewalks are so damaged that there are significant trip and fall hazards. Risk to other's property is perhaps you have potholes in the parking lot that will cause damage to people's vehicles, or a tree branch that needs trimming or likely will fall on parked cars. It can also be something as simple as the door locks don't work and renter's property may be stolen.

Once you have analyzed your facility problems (and costs) compared to how you plan to utilize the building, then you can determine what your course of action is.

"Stuff"
An inventory and assessment of all "personal property" is needed as well. This would be everything from furniture and equipment to vehicles (everything other than real estate).

This information is necessary to make decisions on several areas:

- How you will divide the property with the legacy congregation if you are separating them from the Ministry Center.
- Whether you have the necessary property for your Ministry Center, or whether you need to acquire more or different property.
- Identification of property that will be "shared" with tenants (in common areas) or things like office furniture in rooms for rent.
- How much space you are going to have to allocate to storage.
- Whether you have items that can be sold to raise funds.

"Stuff" is a bigger issue than you may realize. At CMC, we had 70 years' worth of "stuff" accumulated all over the building. For five years I have been on a campaign to get rid of junk, and every time I think we can declare ourselves clutter-free, we run across something else. Just recently we got rid of an enormous 50-year-old copy machine in the basement. This machine probably hadn't been used in more than 30 years, and was so big it wouldn't even fit through the door or up the basement stairs without being dismantled. But it had to be disposed of, because we needed to "refresh" the room for a prospective renter. Ergo, this "junk" became a business/finance issue. One other troublesome property issue alone was the dozen old and broken pianos in the building. People think that all church pianos are sacred and valuable, but when they are rusted and broken they are just worthless and a liability. They are unbelievably heavy and cumbersome to move, and even if you get them outside and loaded on a truck, you will probably have to pay a substantial disposal fee.

Although you may think there is no harm in just leaving "stuff" in a corner or storage room, you are going to find out that churches who rent your spaces are going to want not just worship and office space, but storage space as well, so keeping an old piano, or other non-useful items rapidly becomes a business decision.

Category 4: General

Do you have a website; if yes, are you going to have the same webpage URL? At what point will you change from one to another?

Is your insurance adequate, or should anything change?

Appendix L is a list of questions which must be decided before implementation.

Chapter 22: How Do We Become a Ministry Center?
(Implementing)

"The whole point of what we're urging is simply love — love uncontaminated by self-interest and counterfeit faith, a life open to God. Those who fail to keep to this point soon wander off into cul-de-sacs of gossip. They set themselves up as experts on religious issues, but haven't the remotest idea of what they're holding forth with such imposing eloquence." (1 Timothy 1:5-7)

Plan your work and then work your plan
Once you have planned your work, it's time to get on with working your plan.

What Do I Do Now?
Once you have made the necessary decisions about your operations, facilities, financial, and legal issues, only then can you start making an implementation plan.

Transition Strategy
I have thought long and hard about the process of church transitions, and don't see (in 95% of the situations) that this conversion can be performed in a method where you choose a date and then stop doing things in the old manner and start doing things radically differently on that same day. The only time that conceivably might work is if you were starting with a church that was already closed. Presumably you aren't in that situation yet, so it seems the only logical method to approach this conversion is to *gradually transition from old to new.* Consequently, perhaps a phased transition plan that uses a gradual transition process overlapping the old with the new model until it is all consistent with the "new," is probably an implementation strategy to embrace. This may consist of bringing in some new renters while you are still operating in the "old church" model; perhaps using volunteers to fill any current positions should they go empty, etc.

Other Actions: Assemble a Team
If you have gone through the considerations and assessments of the previous pages, you have developed a great deal of information you can use.

You probably had the help of others in the assessments and those people may form the core of who you are going to need to accomplish the transition. The most likely roles are: Team Leader/Project Manager; Financial Advisor; Facilities Advisor; and Legal Advisor. These generally are going to be volunteers, but expect to pay the Legal Advisor.

The most important positions are the Team Leader and the Project Manager – in smaller organizations this likely will be the same person. The Team Leader has to be the visionary and always see the bigger picture on such things as where the project is going; what impact it will have on the denomination and the community; deciding on course corrections when new information comes to light; how synergy can be achieved by partnering with various groups or individuals; performing Public Relations for the project; and keeping their superiors regularly apprised of project status. The Project Manager should be focused on implementing the plan: making sure that each team member is doing their job; that actions are happening in the correct order; ironing out the daily, routine hiccups; and staying on time and on budget.

The characteristics you are looking for in *all* team members are that they are enthusiastic and optimistic *(one pessimistic person drags down the whole group);* and firmly believe that God will help them succeed.

The characteristics/skills most desired in a Team Leader are: visionary; strategic thinker; adaptable; creative/innovative; team builder and leader; decision maker; business person; and communicator. A Project Manager needs to be: focused; organized; a "people person"; and a problem solver. Both have to have a high degree of integrity and a superlative work ethic.

It is better if your Team Leader becomes the first Director of your new organization. It will smooth the transition because you will continue to experience daily hiccups for a while, and they will have intimate knowledge of the history and journey of the organization, as well as contacts and name recognition. Sometimes this won't be possible, but if you have planned for someone other than the Team Leader to be the initial Director, perhaps this person could become a member of the transition Team. It will help them and you in the long run and ensure a higher degree of success.

Get Everyone on the Same Page
Once you have gotten your prospective team members selected, the first act would be to brief the members on the vision of the new organization so everyone starts on the same page. You should have, at least minimally, discussed this with each of your team members when you enlisted them,

but perhaps each had a varying degree of understanding of the big picture, so it is important that you share this information again within the group so all can gain from the questions and input of one another. Generally, you would start by explaining why it was not advantageous or even possible to continue the old organization the way it was going. Then describe the new vision and the benefits it can generate.

Appendices M and N are examples of an organizational model and a revenue stream model respectively. It may help to use graphics like this to convey your new model.

Also, discuss with the team the individual strategic decisions made with them.

Identify a Target Date and Build a Timeline
Now that you have made some key decisions indicating what the new organization should look like and strategies for getting there, it is time to develop a preliminary (broad) timeline with key target dates. Probably the first thing is to identify a desired target date for completion. In a project this size, it may be two or more years out, but it is totally dependent on your unique circumstances. If you have decided on a phased transition, break down the individual tasks that require completion, arrange them into a logical chronological order, and then split them into the most logical phase depending on how long each is expected to take. Your timeline should contain target dates for the start and finish of each phase, and some phases may be overlapping.

Wandering in the Desert
We never had a target date at Christ Ministry Center, we were just doing all the actions necessary "as fast as we could", and we never really had a date when we considered it complete. Altogether, it took ten years, the first half dozen years were spent just in the dreaming and contemplating "what if" phase. We also didn't have a clear understanding of what our approval chain of command was (neither did they); or what the administrative/paperwork would consist of, or how long that would take. As it turned out, the denominational approval took about two years because we all were in unexplored territory and it kept getting kicked back to us to answer more questions as our superiors were being wise to tread lightly. (We were already pretty much operating in the new model by then, but we hadn't legitimatized it with the official paperwork.) When the corporation paperwork was filed with the Secretary of State, it took more than eight months (we were a 100+ year old corporation that had not been kept up to

date); and the tax exemption 501(c)(3) IRS Form 1023 approval took almost another year due to the voluminous backlog at the IRS – the actual processing took a few weeks, the rest of the time was waiting for it to make it to the top of some tax reviewer's desk. If you have done your preliminary research, your process shouldn't take nearly as long.

Chapter 23: How Can Church Management Become Dynamic?
(Managing)

"I know you inside and out, and find little to my liking. You're not cold, you're not hot — far better to be either cold or hot! You're stale. You're stagnant. You make me want to vomit. You brag, 'I'm rich, I've got it made, I need nothing from anyone,' oblivious that in fact you're a pitiful, blind beggar, threadbare and homeless. The people I love, I call to account — prod and correct and guide so that they'll live at their best. Up on your feet, then! About face! Run after God!" (Revelations 3:15-17)

Most seminaries require a course, "Church Administration 101". Seminarians usually do not see themselves as church administrators. After all, we were called to preach, teach, counsel, evangelize and change the world; not plan budgets, manage staffs or attend committee meetings.

One pastor said, *"They taught me in seminary to preach sermons, serve communion, perform weddings and funerals, baptize believers, conduct pastoral counseling and visit the sick, not be the CEO of a non-profit organization."*

At the beginning of our call and career, we just don't see how managing the church is an important part of our job. But it doesn't take long to discover ministers spend at least half their time in church management.

I was no different. I barely recall the "Church Admin 101" course at Southern Seminary, probably because I slept through most of it. No matter how hard the professor tried to prepare us for this vital role of ministry, most of us found the subject matter to be boring.

Something happened to change my attitude toward church management. My early pastorates exposed how ill-prepared I was to manage a church. Most ministers wish we had paid a bit more attention in the "Church Admin 101" course! By the time I began my doctoral dissertation in 1985, I wrote *"...the church, by virtue of its nature as an organization, must be managed."* The dissertation was my first attempt to share how we may all become better church managers using technology. In hindsight it was both primitive by todays' standard, but also prophetic.

What changed between "Church Admin 101" and the dissertation? Here are the things I discovered and continue to learn.

First, Anchor Management in Ministry

Realize that church management becomes dynamic when it is rooted in the mission of the local church. It is not something extra that has to be done, but something essential to the vitality of ministry. If church leaders see administration as a necessary evil, much like taking out the garbage, then it will be exactly that – boring and dreaded. When church leaders discover administration is a valuable means to lead, guide and transform the church, it takes on a whole new dynamic and perspective.

Notice I avoid saying church management is "easy". And until it becomes dynamic, it isn't much fun either. For me now, by connecting church management with ministry, both have become easier and exciting.

Second, Don't Micro-Manage

Some clergy are "control freaks". They want to police everything that happens under their roof. That leads to inefficiency, ineffectiveness and ultimately burnout.

I love the story of how Jethro, Moses' father-in-law, corrected Moses' management style. Moses thought he was being a good leader by hearing every complaint the Children of Israel had. Long lines formed from dawn to dusk waiting to tell Moses their complaint. Jethro said, *"What you are doing is not good. You and the people with you will wear yourselves out, for the thing is too heavy for you; you are not able to perform it alone."* *(Exodus 18:17-18).*

Trying to do it all yourself, or control everything under your roof, will surely limit what the church manager and members can accomplish. And sooner than later, you and your congregation will "wear yourselves out".

That is not to say you should adopt the "laissez-faire" or hands off approach to management. But when you learn to delegate, trust others and form alliances, you will be surprised at how much more gets accomplished.

Every member comes fully equipped with a variety of gifts and graces. Too often, we do not allow them to use those gifts and graces doing what God intends them do within the church.

Management become dynamic when you learn it's not all up to you, when you discover the compounded impact of your members' and partner's gifts and graces, and when you see the hand of God at work in your daily life and ministry.

Third, Manage More, Do Less

I knew you would like this one! In the business world, workers who excel at a particular skill get promoted to management. Often they fail. Why is it, for instance, the best programmer in the world fails as technology manager? That is simply because there is a critical distinction between "doing" and "managing". If managers spend their time "doing" the things that got them promoted, they are not "managing". The things managers "do" are different than the things non-management staffers "do".

To be clear, managers "do" as much, if not more, than "doers". But the things managers do are management tasks.

You would be shocked to see an Admiral swabbing the deck of a ship. He or she might love swabbing the deck, and may in truth be the greatest deck "swabber" in the world. But the Navy needs Admirals to lead, guide, envision, manage and prepare the Navy to accomplish its mission.

The same holds true in the church. Many churches close because no one is leading! We need clergy and church leaders to lead.

When you discover church management is a tool for leadership, it will become dynamic.

Fourth, Practice "Centergy"

A basic difference between a church and a Ministry Center is the model that forms the foundation. Our model is not the only one, and we invite you to borrow, adapt, and build upon our model so it fits your setting.

Once we adopted the Ministry Center Model and began managing CMC using it as the foundation, we noticed a synergy (which we call "Centergy") began to emerge. This is where the dynamic aspect of management appeared. Suddenly, the whole became greater than the sum of its parts.

To illustrate, since we have basic ministries such as food, clothing, shelter, counseling, wellness, and welcoming strangers, one of our strategic partners, Welcome Home Ministries (WHM), a women's incarceration and re-entry ministry, suggested we form a joint ministry for women re-entering society after incarceration. The most critical point for a woman re-entering society is when she is released. With no support system in place, and when family and friends have abandoned her, she is most likely to return to the habits and environment that got her in jail. That increases recidivism (the revolving door at the jail). But by partnering with Welcome Home Ministries, CMC is now the "first stop" for women coming out of jail. WHM provides the expertise and counsel. CMC provides the basic necessities (food, clothes, etc.) to help the ladies start a new life. Neither WHM nor CMC could do this alone, but we can provide an amazing ministry together. That's Centergy!

God brings people and organizations to us almost daily. Every new "dot" (ministry or organization) provides exciting new dynamics for touching lives for Christ's sake. It's is both exciting and rewarding to "connect the dots". And if such dynamics don't enliven church management, I am not sure what can.

Church management through "Centergy" is dynamic. By connecting the dots, CMC's critical mass grows. More dots emerged offering more connections. It's organic progression.

Fifth, "Take authority in the church"
When I was ordained an elder, Bishop Marshall Meadors laid his hands upon my head and said, "take authority in the church". Every Methodist clergy hears those words. It does not mean become an authoritarian dictator. It means to lead and manage the church using the gifts God has provided.

Taking authority requires both courage and wisdom. As an institution, the church is resistant to change. Yet other than taxes and death, change is the only absolute reality in this life. Every leader must decide if he or she will wait for change to overtake us, or take charge of change. It may require rocking the boat a bit, something that may make the Church Council or District Superintendent uncomfortable. But taking authority means we must do our job in managing the church.

When leaders lead, management becomes dynamic.

Sixth, Expect and Attempt Great Things
William Carey (1761-1834) once proclaimed, *"Expect great things from God; Attempt great things for God."* An old proverb says, *"Blessed are they who expect nothing, for they shall not be disappointed."*

No one is more critical to the dynamic management of a local church than the leader. If the leader does not expect God can use the church, or attempt to do great and mighty things, then surely not much will happen other than the "same old, same old". This requires faith; even the size of a mustard seed which has power to move mountains. My grandmother's favorite saying was, *"Can't never could do anything!"*

Here again, when church management and ministry are separate, this disconnect will hinder both management and ministry.

Seventh, Join Hands
No, I'm not about to ask us to all sing "Kumbaya". What I have learned much too late in life is the power in strategic alliances. There is only so much one can do. Ecclesiastes 4:9 says, *"Two are better than one; because they have a good reward for their labor."*

In my management of CMC, I see two circles of partners and alliances. The first circle includes those churches and charities closest to us. That includes Welcome Home Ministries. Recently, I discovered a wider circle that includes all the organizations in San Diego whose focus is upon re-entry into society after incarceration. Similarly, I have joined an alliance of organizations focused upon immigrants' rights and social justice. By meeting the community leaders who head these wonderful organizations (some religious, some not), we strengthen the efforts of each other.

Nothing is more dynamic than seeing individuals and organizations uniting to help the helpless.

Essential Wisdom
Managing the church requires attending committee meetings, preparing budgets, writing reports, repairing broken toilets, fund raising, and a host of other chores for which the minister is ultimately responsible. The Ministry Center model offers a way to connect ministry and management in a way both become more efficient and effective, bringing a dynamic that will otherwise never exist.

Rusty's Salvation
Nothing is more rewarding and invigorating than to realize you have made a difference for good in someone's life. That's when management and ministry converge to become dynamic. I have known Rusty Crumm for at least a decade, probably longer. He was one of the organizers and leaders of "The Wall", a 12-step program that met every weekday afternoon at Christ United Methodist for years.

A couple years ago, for a variety of reasons, the group moved to another location, but Rusty and I kept in touch. He is kind to respond to my Pastorgraphs from time to time. Rusty did so in a way that warmed my heart and brought tears to my eyes. I am grateful Rusty gave me permission to share his testimony with you with minor edits.

"Hi Pastor Bill, since The Wall moved from CMC (Christ Ministry Center) we've been on life support, as well. We had a business meeting [3 of us] last week and decided since we couldn't be fully self-supporting in paying rent we had to discontinue. In addition to not being able to pay rent, most of our leading members' schedules changed and we weren't able to keep the doors open. Also, due to health issues I haven't been able to attend meetings regularly too.

However, I was secretary of the Tuesday 4 o'clock meeting and I am committed to keeping that meeting going. Funny thing is that was my first services commitment at the Wall 14 years ago, as Tuesday secretary at CMC. **It saved my life along with a bunch of other individuals who struggle with addictions. I can't tell you how many individuals got clean, found God, and their lives are on a whole different path because of The Wall and CMC.** *Unfortunately, many more weren't able to surrender and they have died or continue to suffer.*

Another sad commentary is NA (Narcotics Anonymous) serves the sick and hopeless who have nowhere else to go and for that our image isn't one of hope and change to outsiders. Don't know why I'm sharing this with you besides to share with you God's work isn't always obvious, especially those less fortunate to work with the sick, poor, and discarded. I am a blessed man to see God's work daily in my life and others. Thank you for allowing The Wall to use CMC and I'm sure you took your share of criticism for serving the sick as well. God bless and continue your work at CMC.

~Rusty"

When I talk about the ministries at CMC, I tend to overlook the 12 step groups. Rusty's testimony is a reminder that urban ministry must involve caring for both the body and soul of those our society "discards". In many ways, caring for the physical needs is the easier part: providing groceries, clothing, shelter and basic needs. Meeting the spiritual needs is less obvious. Often it happens without fanfare. It may begin with a simple hug, offering acceptance the dispossessed may not have experienced in years.

Maybe it happens when we provide a welcome or a place to come and talk with God.

Not long after Rusty wrote this message, God brought his NA support group back to Christ Ministry Center. They surrendered their old group and experienced resurrection in a new group, bigger and better than any of us could have imagined. Thank you, Lord!

Chapter 24: How Do We Avoid "The Potholes"?
(Navigating)

"Evil people fall into their own traps; good people run the other way, glad to escape." (Proverbs 29:6)

Landlord vs Partner

Since a large portion, if not all of your revenue might come from the churches and charities (or other rentals) that use your building, it is important to not fall into the pothole of simply being a landlord. Anyone may purchase a building or apartment complex and rent space. A Ministry Center is not just a landlord-tenant business arrangement. In a Ministry Center, there should exist a partnership with each group that uses the facilities. That partnership doesn't have to be an elaborate contract. It may be as simple as acknowledging each church and charity is seeking to help people in need, which is the mission of the Ministry Center. The partners provide services to those in need, and the Ministry Center provides a base of operations. That means both are partners in achieving the Ministry Center Model.

Helpful Tips

What tenants want (expect):
All tenants expect:
- Adequate, clean, fully stocked restrooms
- Adequate nearby parking
- Secure, locked spaces
- A mail and delivery pickup area
- Hardwired phone lines
- Wi-Fi (Wireless internet access)
- Adequate signage in prominent places to direct visitors
- Use of meeting rooms
- Some janitorial service (at least in shared spaces)

All church tenants want:
- Worship space
- Office space
- Adequate, exclusive, storage space near their worship space
- Parking suitable for their congregation
- Use of social activity space
- Use of a food preparation space

- Use of a child nursery
- Sunday School classroom spaces
- Projectors in the Worship space
- Exclusive Bulletin Board in a prominent area

All **Charitable Organization tenants** want:
- Office space
- Work space suitable to their mission (e.g., food pantry space, clothes closet space, etc.)
- Use of an area with microwaves, refrigerators, etc. (breakroom)

Partners and MOUs

Partners were mentioned previously, and defined as groups you are supporting in some ways that do not pay you rent. We have several partners at the Ministry Center. One for example, is a women's prison re-entry program, which has designated office space in the building – free because they are inadequately funded, but performing a powerful ministry. Another partner comes into the building twice a week and distributes groceries for a $1/$2 charge (if people can afford it). Those are two examples of partners whom we support because we endorse what they are doing that is core to our mission (and they are 501(c)(3) tax exempt organizations).

We have rental contracts with the people who pay us rent, and that pretty much formalizes our arrangement with them, but then we have Memorandums of Understanding (MOU) with 'partners' like the aforementioned, so we are both clear on what our mutual expectations are. Appendix O is an example.

We have other types of partners, such as organizations that are not on a regular schedule, but come to our building for a day at a time to perform some beneficial service to the community (and who may or may not give us a fee each time). Some examples of those: the city/state using our building as a polling place during elections; a commercial medical screening service which screens for blocked arteries or stroke symptoms; the Blood Mobile; Good Will or other sponsored job fairs; and so forth. I also belong to an immigration alliance and a prison ministry consortium, and they occasionally need a venue to meet with the public, or hold a class and I welcome them to our building for free if it doesn't conflict with our regular schedules.

Any organizations that you have a regular interface with and they provide you some service or you provide them some service, should be formalized with an MOU.

Renters and Rent Rates

Charities and churches love renting space in a church building (more than being in a school or commercial space) because being in a church offers more cachet for them. That is why in a large city like San Diego we seldom lack for tenants and can be somewhat choosy in who we accept. My goal is to accept groups whose mission and purpose mirror/fulfill the Ministry Center's mission; and who could be helped and blessed by affiliating with us. It is always my vision that our "Ministry Center family" would become very synergistic and anyone renting from us would benefit by that. This has worked wonderfully for a number of our organizations such as the half a dozen churches we have that partake in our Friday grocery ministry; or the joint religious services on Christmas and Easter; or the special events we sponsor such as Christmas' Toys for Tots, and choir/musical events; or even when some pastors invite pastors from our other churches to speak at their revivals. To my knowledge, we have never had any issues in any of our churches with 'poaching' members from other churches. And mostly, I have long talks with the prospective renters to make sure they understand they have to be part of a family and are willing to make accommodations with all the other organizations operating within our building.

Rent rates: We have tried some different methods of determining what to charge our various tenants that would be both fair and equitable. At one time (when we had fewer renters) I tried charging a set amount per square foot, but that didn't last long because all of our footage is not 'equal'. Four hundred square feet in the basement is not as desirable as the same amount of space on the first floor. Rental of the Sanctuary at 10:00 a.m. on Wednesday morning is not the same as 10:00 a.m. on Sunday morning. Because we have no handicapped access to the second floor, those spaces are not necessarily as valuable as the same space on the first floor.

Now I use a "gut feel" for determining rents. These are the things I consider for each organization:
- What is their purpose?
- Do they have a 501(c)(3) tax exempt status? *(This is mandatory at CMC)*
- Do they have or can they get $1M in liability insurance? *(This is mandatory at CMC)*
- How many people do they have in their church or organization?

- How much space do they want/need?
- What do we have available?
- Do our available spaces meet their needs?
- Do we have spaces that should/could be coming available?
- What can they reasonably afford without strapping them?
- What are comparable rental rates in our city?
- Is it equitable with what our other tenants are paying?
- Is whatever they are planning to do going to cause significant increases in our utilities?
- Can they be flexible in their service times or other accommodations they are seeking?

I strive to charge all of our renters the least possible (and still be making sound financial decisions), because we are trying to nurture and encourage them in their endeavors. When we are booked solid and bursting at the seams, I frequently lower rents for the ones who have been moved to lesser spaces or who are being impacted more than others by the crowd. I usually tell my wife (and Center's Financial Manager) when I intend to lower someone's rent, and she will caution me if I am getting close to an unwise financial decision.

Scheduling

First, I want to explain that God is the scheduler for our building, all I do is write it down. Every time I think we are absolutely chock-full, God sends someone else to squeeze into a tiny slot that I didn't even realize existed – it's amazing. Appendix P is a sample schedule for our 'shared use areas' and you will see what I mean. When I came to Christ Church, very little of the spaces were being used at all. When we cleaned up the first floor (there had been a nursery occupying most of the area) and brought in new groups, I was pleased by how occupied we were. Then we filled up half of the second floor which hadn't been used in years. When the rest of the second floor was occupied, including any storage or closet spaces, I was positive we were full, until God showed me how wrong I was. He sent a few groups that wanted the basement – which was old, often flooded with our infrequent SoCal rains, and looked like a dungeon. But we managed to clean up the largest basement room and dry it out. Then God let loose his own flood of demand for the rest of the basement – eight more rooms, some of which hadn't had the doors opened in decades. Literally, some doors had been permanently stuck closed by shifting ground and wet conditions, and we had to remove the doors to even get inside. The demand did not stop. When we literally had no empty rooms left, we pushed out to our portico, and cleaned, repaired and painted it to become an outdoor dining area for our renters. Masterful scheduling is key to maximizing your available spaces.

I want to express my eternal gratitude to my wife Anita, who has done so much to whip our building into shape over the last few years. She has not just led work parties, but also put in more than a thousand hours of sweat equity making repairs and remodeling to improve every room and hallway. She personally and singlehandedly painted and repaired more than 20 rooms in our building. I love her, I am proud and in awe of her, and am so grateful for what she has done in helping me achieve God's vision.

Building Rules

When you have so many groups and personalities and many non-English speaking people in the building, you have to have building rules (in several languages). Most of our signs or other written instructions are in English, Spanish, Ethiopian, Haitian, Eritrean, and Kajin Majel (Marshallese). (Thank the Lord for internet translations.) We tend to make these rules an attachment to our rental contracts. I have attached a sample of building rules as Appendix J.

Utilities

I only mention utilities as a reminder that the more groups you have in your building, the more your utilities are going to increase. Your utilities may double or triple in changing from a standard church to changing to a Ministry Center. Some groups use more utilities than others.

Water

We have one group for example, that brought in their own portable baptistery, which looks something like a hot tub on wheels. We are in a severe drought in California, and if you fill that baptistery frequently, it makes a difference on the water bill. Our water bills were outrageous for several cycles, and we did everything we could to find the root cause (had a leak specialist come out, put locks on our outside spigots and so forth), but the bills kept soaring. We finally discovered that we had "water thieves" who had defeated our locks and were stealing thousands of gallons of our water every month. These were probably marijuana growers who steal the water they need for their plants because they don't want to alert the water company to unreasonably high usage, because that in turn alerts the police.

Also, people don't necessarily treat the facilities the way you would like them to. Too many times people leave faucets running, or have the air conditioners going full blast with all the doors open. It is a constant battle to educate your tenants. One of the things we did to minimize the water bill was to change out all our oldest (some 40 years old) toilets that were using six gallons or more per flush, for modern low-flow toilets that use less than two gallons.

Garbage

I don't want to leave this topic without speaking about what I refer to as our 'garbage wars'. Of course when your tenants increase, so does your garbage. We pay the disposal company hundreds of dollars a month for service. We not only had to increase our number of dumpsters, but also increased the number of pickups per week.

The neighbors don't like to look at our dumpsters. Wherever we located them, they were always visible to some neighbors. To keep the peace, we built a fairly attractive (and expensive) enclosure around the dumpsters with a gate on it. Unfortunately, those neighbors who don't want to look at our garbage, are the same neighbors that make "midnight donations" of their large junk/refuse, and overflow our dumpsters. When the dumpsters overflow, the trash service company not only refuses to pick them up, but charges us an "overflow" penalty fee. And the garbage overflow attracts rats, so we pay even more for our exterminating service to put out rat traps around the garbage area as well.

Then we put locks on the dumpster barn, which is highly inconvenient for the hundreds of people who are in our building every week, and that helped eliminate some of the unauthorized use, but a number of our midnight visitors would still throw their refuse over the 6' fence on top of the dumpsters, or some just pile it up on the outside of the fence so you can't even get to the gate. We put a security camera on the area, so we know what is happening, but even if we recognize the offenders, there is really nothing to be done about it.

I would like to provide advice about this but the only thing I can say is *"This is rubbish!"*

Chapter 25: What Are "The Lessons Learned"?
(Learning)

"Put the question to our ancestors, study what they learned from their ancestors. For we're newcomers at this, with a lot to learn, and not too long to learn it. So why not let the ancients teach you, tell you what's what, instruct you in what they knew from experience? (Job 8:8-10)

Lessons Learned and Other Helpful Advice
Most urban Ministry Centers will find some conflicts and rough spots but that doesn't mean you are doing something wrong.

Neighborhood Relations
If your Ministry Center is located in a residential area, one of the first things you will discover is that the neighbors may not be as benevolent as you and your partners in meeting the needs of those in need. Unfortunately, their attitude is based more on economics than compassion. To put it bluntly, they may say, *"There goes the neighborhood!"* This is especially true if you have homeless, hungry, hurting and helpless people coming "on site" to receive services. Neighbors may see a potential threat to both their "property value" and personal safety. But Jesus did not say feed and care for those in need "if the neighbors don't complain".

It may take years to develop trust with the neighbors. What we experienced was that by inviting the neighbors in for special events, including a neighborhood meeting with city officials over another common concern, they saw CMC was making the neighborhood a better place by helping those in need. It is important to communicate with the neighborhood, and for the neighbors to see the Ministry Center as a community resource. One of our most vocal critics silenced herself when she started receiving groceries through our food ministry. CMC is the neighborhood voting precinct. We invite neighbors to our grocery distribution, job fair, health screenings, Thanksgiving meal, and to all our worship services.

Sad truths
(This falls under the category of "be patient, trusting, kind and generous, but not foolish")

1. Some "Street people":
   - Can be unpredictable and dangerous, even when you are helping them
   - Can easily become violent

- May vandalize and steal from your building
- Can be a danger to your staff and other tenants

Although many people living on the streets are good hearted, not all are. Also, many suffer from various forms of mental illness. This sometimes makes helping them difficult. In our urban neighborhood, there are numerous street people who visit the Ministry Center every day. When my wife is working in the building she always has pepper spray (and usually a box cutter or some other tool within reach). Our Office Manager is the kindest and most generous person you could ever hope to meet, but she has a Taser in her desk drawer. I am 6'5" and 300 pounds, but my family gave me a container of pepper spray after a homeless man physically attacked me when I told him he had to leave the building because he was drunk and exposing himself. *(Fortunately, I just got scratches.)* But be careful, and always try to remember God's command to love the unlovable – even when they are cursing you or trying to hurt you.

2. Some churches who rent your spaces:
- Will tear up God's building
- Will deny they are responsible for damages even when you have it on videotape
- Will lie to your face
- Will crank up their sound systems until the neighbors call the police
- Will leave a filthy mess after they have used a space
- Will disrespect the other churches in the building
- Will not pay their rent on time

We like to think that people who are affiliated with a church are a cut above the average and will display Christian values and behavior. It pains me to say this, but some groups are just disrespectful to the building, to the neighbors, to the other tenants, and to you and your staff. They allow their children to run all over unattended, tear up the furniture and carve up the pews. They break all the Building Rules, and then deny it when you call them in for a discussion. I am accused of being too trusting and forgiving by my wife, but this is why she put a "60 days' release clause" in our contracts. Either party can break the contract and leave with sixty days' (or sometimes less) notice. Sadly, we have had to ask some groups to leave because they couldn't or wouldn't try to fit in with our "Ministry Center family" or abide by building policies.

3. Some people will try to take advantage of you, and mistake your kindness for weakness. I always try to be kind and give people second, third, fourth and even more chances, as the Bible tells us to do. Every minister knows some people will come to your office and deliver a sob story trying to get money (usually for cigarettes or drugs); or have some kind of con game they want to run on you. Beware of people who have some great (religious and/or charitable) idea for making and sharing with you copious amounts of money; and especially beware of people who come in with their grand plan to enrich the Ministry Center. I have learned through experience that every contract has to be reviewed by my wife (who is a contracting professional), despite how sincere and trustworthy the pitchman appears. All this is to say, *"Beware of wolves in sheep's clothing."*

4. Somedays you will feel like all you do is fix broken toilets. It's not just the toilets, it's the electrical, the roof leaks, broken locks, the sinks, the pews, and virtually anything and everything. There is a price to pay for 'using every square inch of the building' and it comes in the form of wear and tear on the building and its appurtenances. I say toilets because we have 20+ toilets and urinals in our 70-year-old building, and we are putting our plumber's dozen children through college on our business alone. And that is just for the major repairs. My wife, our custodian, our handy man, and our sexton all work on the easier plumbing repairs. Even our Office Manager has become adept at clearing blockages in sinks and toilets and shutting off the water in moments of utter crisis. (And we have all had a lesson from my wife on how to use the utility pump to dry up the rain flooded basement.)

It is easy to become discouraged when you are working on spiritual matters or preparing for a meeting with the bishop, or a prospective partner, and people come rushing into your office to announce the latest building repair "crisis". At those times, all you can do is take a deep breath and say, *"Jesus, thank you that we have a building where we can reach so many others and make a difference in their lives (and I might need your help for this problem".)*

This all is to say that being the Ministry Center Director is not for the impatient or faint-hearted. There are inevitable negative aspects to operating a Ministry Center, and not every day is all sunshine and inspiration. But no matter how much I may get frustrated with the daily aches and pains, I am instantly restored and renewed whenever a precious little toddler stumbles out of the nursery across from my office, and stops in my doorway to give me a timid little wave and a big smile. Then I remember the big picture and know that God is present and blessing our efforts.

Chapter 26: What Role Does Technology Play?
(Progressing)

"It takes wisdom to build a house, and understanding to set it on a firm foundation; It takes knowledge to furnish its rooms with fine furniture and beautiful draperies. It's better to be wise than strong; intelligence outranks muscle any day. Strategic planning is the key to warfare; to win, you need a lot of good counsel." (Proverbs 24:3-6)

My doctoral dissertation, completed in 1985, stressed two points: (1), that the church, by its nature as an organization must be managed (see Chapter 23); and (2), that technology can (and should) be used to help church leaders manage and minister within the church.

Keep in mind that in the early to mid-1980s, desktop computing was in its infancy. There was no internet, and only a few "networks" where large mainframe computers could "talk" to each other. Certainly churches could not afford the computers available then, even if they had staff who knew how to operate them. IBM at that time saw desktop computing as a fad, or maybe even a threat to their large room-size computers. My doctoral dissertation committee at Columbia Seminary all but laughed at my premise that one day, desktop computers would play an important role in churches and ministry.

If this sounds like "I told you so," please know I hesitate to call attention to the embarrassingly primitive technology available at the time. I was using a Radio Shack "micro" computer with the first database application ever developed for desktop computers, written by a friend in Atlanta.

Thirty years later, churches are still among the last institutions to embrace technology. A recent review of churches in the California Pacific Conference of The United Methodist Church revealed a surprising number of churches had no church office access to technology. In fact, some churches expressed resistance to offers of donated computers. That passive resistance greatly hinders the denomination's ability to communicate in a more efficient and effective manner and hampers our "connectional system".

There are several reasons for the passive attitude to technology in many churches. First, most ministers are not trained in technology, nor do they necessarily have an aptitude for it. Second, even though the cost of computers has fallen as fast as their power has increased, computing is still expensive when you take into consideration the overall hardware, software, security and bandwidth costs. (Churches are not called "nonprofit" by accident!)

In my tri-vocational career, technology has been a constant. Being a radio announcer in high school and college exposed me to broadcasting technology, news teletype machines, live sporting events patched in from hundreds of miles away, and so on. That was amazing technology for a dusty Delta town in the late 1960s. A few years later, how fortunate I was to be in Atlanta when the micro-computer revolution exploded. My appetite for technology and my adaptability to the constant changes in hardware and software has served me well for over a half century!

Mostly self-taught in computing; I enrolled in post-graduate computer science courses at NASA's Stennis Space Center through the University of Southern Mississippi. That formal training enabled me to both become a technology operations manager at a large Southern California utility for over a decade and teach technology management courses at San Diego State University (and at other San Diego colleges) and of course, this is not the usual path of most ordained clergy, especially in The United Methodist Church.

All this is to say that technology can be a strategic ally in church management, and critical in operating a Ministry Center. But from this background and perspective, I offer the following advice and guidance for using technology in church management, especially for a Ministry Center.

With computer hardware and software getting more powerful every year, it would be foolish for me to make specific recommendations. That advice would be obsolete by the time you read it. However, I recommend most churches consider the following. Please note some of these are free to use, and others modestly priced with huge returns on investment or productivity.

Website and Social Media
Gone are the days when people locate a church using the Yellow Pages. A web presence is essential in today's world. That includes a webpage and some form of social media, such as Facebook or Twitter. And they better evoke a positive impression, because your website and social media has replaced your "curb appeal" for new members. This could very well be someone's first (and last) impression of your church!

Your website should present at least the basic information regarding your church; its location with map, times of services, mission, staff, programs, etc. Your social media (Facebook, Twitter, etc.) is best for telling short stories of your church's activities with pictures, music, or other media. Personally I find Facebook essential for communication in today's environment. Your website and social media should link to each other, allowing visitors to easily navigate between them.

It is no longer necessary to have programming skills to have a professional website. A computer novice can create an attractive web presence with a tool like Wix.com for free. (The free version will place ads on your site, but a modest paid version will remove the ads.)

"Content is King"
Think of your social media posts as commercials for your church or Ministry Center. Where else can you tell your story for free with the potential to reach so many people?

While the church website is a more permanent resource, please know that when you give birth to a website, just like a baby, your website needs a lot of tender love and care. No one will come back time after time to visit your website if the content never changes! I often see church websites that have not been updated in years. That communicates volumes to your site visitors. There is a simple "counter" that can be placed on your website. This can help you know how many people visit or revisit your website, and tell you how you are doing keeping up with fresh content and useful information.

It is easier to show the life of your congregation through Facebook. You should make at least three new "posts" a week to show things are happening at your church. Otherwise, you communicate that "nothing is happening here", a message you don't want your "followers" to get.

Church Newsletter
The printed church newsletter is rapidly going the way of the dinosaur. The time, effort and cost of printing and mailing old-fashioned printed newsletters (which usually go straight into the garbage can) are easily offset by e-newsletters.

Services such as MailChimp and ConstantContact allow you to produce professional looking e-newsletters for free (up to a certain point). Plus, these services make sure you are in compliance with federal regulations, including an "unsubscribe" feature for anyone who does not wish to receive your newsletter any longer.

A word to the wise: My childhood pastor and lifelong mentor, the Rev. Harold A. Shirley, once told me the clergy column in the church newsletter should "say something". What he meant is it should not be a place for the pastor to promote the Wednesday night pot-luck supper or appeal for more choir members. It should be a place to share a message from his or her heart. When church newsletters simply promote the "same-old, same-old" they go directly into the garbage can or are quickly deleted from the inbox! In my weekly Pastorgraphs, I try to convey something near and dear to my heart, rather than simply regurgitating the "church announcements".

Streaming Media
Why technology? Consider a church that has 70 people in the sanctuary for worship has the potential to reach 700 or 7,000 people via the web. The equipment and costs to "live stream" your morning worship is amazingly affordable now. But anyone can capture the choir anthem or children's sermon on a smartphone and post it on Facebook before the members get home from worship.

Keep in mind, however, that what you post says more about your church than you realize. Make sure the quality is as good as possible.

Wi-Fi
The public today expects to have Wi-Fi access everywhere: the coffee shop, restaurants, and even church. Wi-Fi can be a blessing and a curse.

Having a strong Wi-Fi system centrally located in your church or Ministry Center eliminates the expense of running computer cables all over your facilities and maintaining that cabling. However, I suggest you give access only to those who really need it, such as church and charity leaders, but not to the general public. You can hide the name of your Wi-Fi so not everyone can discover it. Plus, you should not publish the password to access the Wi-Fi. We found that otherwise, people will park next to your building and use your bandwidth for "God only knows what". Or, if you are located in a residential area, you may be granting free internet access for the neighborhood, while you get stuck with the bandwidth charges, and slow connectivity. Wi-Fi is needed not only in your offices, but in your conference rooms and in the sanctuary so your ministers can connect when they need to show something from the internet on the projectors – which relates to the next topic.

Projectors

Your worship area(s) will most likely require a projection system today. This is so much more cost effective than using printed worship bulletins and hymnals. Some argue that "overhead projection" is making worship less deeply rooted in theology and hymns. Of course, you may use projection for the words of the most formal liturgy and classical hymns as well as contemporary worship's praise songs. Either way, expect that when you become a Ministry Center, the worship spaces will need projection technology.

Electronic Records

Word Processing revolutionized the way everyone handles records. No longer do church office workers have a typewriter and mimeograph machines. Using electronic records for things such as committee minutes and financial records helps save paper, making your office more environmentally responsible. Also, electronic records reduce the space needed to store papers in filing cabinets. Placing those electronic records where they may be accessed over the web (see below) increases efficiency. Locating files electronically is much easier than the old manual search.

Recently, we gathered up 110 "banker's boxes" of paperwork that had accumulated in our building, some going back over 100 years to our parent churches in downtown San Diego. Combined, they took up space in two rooms. After carefully going through these boxes, we discarded the records that had no useful or historical value. We scanned the remaining records, totaling 10,000 pages, into electronic files as text-searchable portable data format (PDF) files. Those two records storage rooms now are being used for other useful purposes.

Citrix "GoTo's" and other Cloud Services

Personally, I find two Citrix products indispensable: GoToMyPC and GoToMeeting.

GoToMyPC allows me to connect to my home computer from anywhere in the world. No more forgetting to bring a certain file to the Church Council meeting. I simply log onto my home computer from my office and print the file to my church office printer across the internet.

Apple and Microsoft also provide "cloud" storage services. They allow you to save all your important files on their servers somewhere out there on the internet, called "the cloud", which you can then securely access and edit, no matter where you are or what computer you are using.

Citrix's GoToMeeting allows you to conduct online meetings with shared video screens and conference call technology. In fact, now, with Voice Over Internet Protocol (VOIP), most virtual meeting participants do not need a phone. Using the computers' microphone, speakers and camera, all participants can see, hear and speak to all the other attendees.

Why have your church leaders make dozens of trips to the church for meetings when some of them can be done online? Why should a District Superintendent or Bishop spend hundreds of hours in "windshield time" to meet with distant ministers and church leaders? Some meetings must be in person, but not all.

Applications
Most computers come with core applications installed, such as Microsoft Office. You pay extra for these applications, such as Word, Excel and PowerPoint. Spreadsheets such as Excel can help you simply set up tables of data for anything you need to make, including financial information and budgets. With a bit of experience, you can manipulate the data to reveal information that may not be apparent.

There are complete software applications you may purchase exclusively for financial data. These help you analyze financial data, print reports and even produce checks. This sort of application reduces the labor time being expended and errors inherent in manual financial record keeping and calculations.

We use Excel to keep track of income and bills to be paid. Good financial management not only tracks income, but projects how cash flow will meet upcoming expenses in the short to mid-term future.

Security Software
Whatever you do, please keep your computer and other technology devices protected and up-to-date with anti-virus and anti-malware applications. If you keep member information (especially birthdays and addresses) on church related computers, you may be liable for damages if that information falls into the hands of "hackers". Computer security software is essential, and must be kept current with daily updates from vendors such as Norton and McAfee.

Security Cameras

Security cameras can eliminate the cost of having security personnel onsite, walking the grounds.

One of the most beneficial investments we made at Christ Ministry Center was a 16-camera security system. With 26,000 square feet in a building that is a "7-day-a-week church", the security cameras are strategically placed to cover every point of entrance into the building. Two cameras cover the parking area, and one covers the front lawn.

Being able to check in and view both live and recorded events from anywhere in the world is a huge management benefit. Thank goodness we have had few incidents, but when something is stolen or damaged, the added layer of security provided by the security cameras is well worth the investment.

Conclusion

As technology continues to improve, so will the benefits to churches and church leaders who embrace and use it as an extension of ministry and church management. On my smartphone, I can view live video of our security cameras, push out the weekly e-newsletter, place a call to a member, post a picture of church events on Facebook, conduct a virtual online meeting, or log onto my home computer. Hello church, it's time for us all to work smarter, being better stewards of both time and money.

SECTION FIVE: Ministry "Centergy"

Chapter 27: The Fount of Blessings
(Blessing)

*"Come, thou Fount of every blessing, tune my heart to sing thy grace;
streams of mercy, never ceasing, call for songs of loudest praise."
(Rev. Robert Robinson, 1757)*

"Wouldn't It Be Nice, If Someone…"

In early 2013, I attended two ministers' meetings, two days apart. One was an ecumenical gathering and the second was a Methodist meeting, both for clergy and faith leaders serving in the Mid-City area of San Diego. At both meetings, each participant shared their church's outreach ministries to help the poor in our community.

At both meetings, someone said, "Wouldn't it be nice if someone would collect the information, print it out, and bring it to our next meeting so we could refer to it when people show up on our doorstep seeking assistance!" We all agreed it would be nice. Then we had a prayer and adjourned.

I had heard the "Wouldn't it be nice" idea when attending meetings of non-profit charity directors and even an interfaith meeting convened by a mayor.

God impressed upon me that collecting the information and distributing it in a printout was not wise. First, only those who had the printout would benefit from the data. Second, the information would soon be out of date. There should be a way of making the data available to everyone and a way to keep the information accurate and current. Obviously, putting the information online via a website database was a better solution.

The only problem was who should we get to create this website and begin collecting the information? Ideally, it should be someone with a background in both ministry and technology, and perhaps someone recently retired who had at least a few hours a week to devote to making it happen.

It didn't take long for me to realize God was asking me to take on this opportunity. To whom much is given, much is required.

Naming It

I name everything. In 4-H, I named all 100 baby chickens that were my project for the county fair. I name the rooms in our building rather than refer to them by their number. So if I was to undertake this project, it needed a name.

Since each service provided by the churches, charities and social agencies are a "blessing" to those who need the services, I recalled the old hymn, "Come Thou Fount of Every Blessing". It works, because each service provider is a "Fount of Blessings" and each service provided is a "Stream of Mercy, Never Ceasing".

What is "The Fount"?

The Fount of Blessings ("The Fount") is a free, user-friendly website (MyFount.com). The Fount contains a searchable database where anyone can find assistance (such as food, clothing, shelter) offered by churches, charities, or social agencies in their local area.

Using the imagery of "Founts" and "Streams", a Fount is a church, charity or organization that offers any form of help to those in need. "Streams" are the services (food, clothing, shelter, etc.) the Fount offers. In short, it connects people in need with free or low cost help in their community.

"The Fount" focuses on those caring ministries mentioned in Matthew 25: 35-37 (food, water, clothing, medical care, prison ministries, and refugee and immigrant services) as well as resources for shelter, employment, training, spiritual support, counseling, recovery groups, women and children, veterans, etc. This is a perfect complement to the Ministry Center.

How "The Fount" Works

Using a map interface, the website user sees a map with a push-pin icon for every Fount in the database. The user can search to filter out all but the specific service they are seeking, such as food. Then the user can zoom into the neighborhood closest to them where that Stream is being offered. By clicking on the push-pin icon, the user sees accurate and timely data about when, where and how the Fount offers that particular Stream.

Developing "The Fount"

I saw right away the potential for databases to revolutionize how we do almost everything. My doctoral dissertation dealt with how ministers can use databases and technology to better manage their ministries.

It was a "God thing" when I met Ken Darois in San Diego. He was my student at San Diego State. I was so impressed with his programming skills I hired him to work for the utility company where I was technology operations manager. He continued to amaze me with his programming skills. After we both left the utility, we maintained contact and worked on several projects together in our spare time.

I shared the idea of creating a website database where both help providers (such as pastors and social workers) and those seeking help (the homeless, poor and hurting) can find help right at their fingertips. Ken, a dedicated Christian himself, agreed to create "The Fount of Blessings" website and database.

God impressed upon me there was a universal need for a resource such as The Fount providing:

- **Online availability**. Unlike notebooks and printed lists which are available only to those who have access to them, anyone can access a database via the web or smartphones.
- **7/24/365 availability.** Churches, charities and social agencies can be contacted only during office hours and on weekdays. "The Fount" information is available seven days a week, 24 hours a day, and 365 days a year.
- **Free to Use.** There is no charge for using "The Fount". Both those needing help and those providing help can connect quickly to more resources via "The Fount" without charge.
- **Easy to Use.** "The Fount" was designed to be user-friendly. The intuitive interface allows even the most inexperienced user to search for help by simply typing a keyword (such as food, clothing, shelter), or use an advanced search to "drill down" to find specific services offered in a local area or on a certain date.
- **Accurate information.** Fount Partners have their own portal into "The Fount" to maintain their Fount and Streams information.
- **Efficient and Effective.** Service providers can see what other ministries and services are available (and when and where) so they are able to reduce duplication or refer their clients to other resources which they don't provide.
- **Confidentiality.** People in need can research online possible resources they desire without having to identify themselves or what they need.

Pilot Project: San Diego

The pilot project for "The Fount" Project was San Diego in 2014. We collected publicly available data about churches, charities and social service agencies and the services they offered. Anyone then can go to the website and search for the help they need most, such as food, clothing, employment help or health services. The Fount has undergone numerous revisions and improvements.

2015: Going Nationwide

In 2015, The Fount has been expanded into all 50 states. The goal for 2016 and beyond is to have the major service providers in each of the major metropolitan areas become "Founts" and share their "Streams of Mercy" with anyone seeking help. My dream is to establish and populate The Fount in every mid-to-large city in the United States. Imagine how beneficial that would be for every city and its people.

Using The Fount at The Ministry Center

Christ Ministry Center uses The Fount to be more effective and efficient in ministry. When someone arrives on our doorstep seeking food, clothing or other services, and if we do not provide those services or have the needed items immediately available, we search The Fount to find another Fount/organization nearby that does provide the services. It's a win-win!

You Can Help

Most cities in The Fount are not as well populated data-wise as San Diego. If you want to populate (with helping services) a specific city, please contact us (info@myfount.com or 888-282-6367) and we will teach you how. Even if you just want to add your own services to The Fount, we can assist you with that also.

Become a Fount or "Virtual Ministry Center"

Since The Fount uses the same model as the Ministry Center Model, any church, charity or social agency, or an individual, can become a "Virtual Ministry Center" using the Fount of Blessings. You can search The Fount for any service needed to help someone at no cost but a few minutes of your time. Imagine having that knowledge at your fingertips and how much more you will be able to help others. We will be more than happy to discuss how your church can use The Fount, become a Fount, or help manage the Fount of Blessings in your community.

"The Fount" is more than a website. It has the potential to become a revolutionary new way for churches, charities and social agencies to work together in providing help for those in need. As government budgets for social programs decline, it is imperative that helping organizations become more efficient and effective, reducing duplication of efforts and missed opportunities to help the helpless, homeless, hurting and hungry in our community.

The Fount can multiply the effectiveness of your church one hundred fold! There is no need to turn away any individual with absolutely no help or assistance. If The Fount is populated in your city, you will always be able to find an organization to which you may refer a person so they can receive the help they need.

The Homeless Hero

"I wish I had met you about two years ago", Tom the Marine said to us one Thursday afternoon at Miramar. "Why is that?" we asked. "Because two years ago, I was living out of my car and could have really used The Fount to locate some things I desperately needed back then."

I was speechless. Standing before me was a handsome young man in his military attire. I could not begin to visualize him as homeless. Tom is now a Marine aviation engineer who works on America's military jets, making sure we are prepared to defend our nation and freedoms. Nearby over the course of the afternoon, at least two dozen of those jets Tom works on took off, often flying in precision formation. Those pilots depend on Tom's training and skills to keep our air fleet in tip-top operating condition.

Again, not so long ago, Tom the aviation engineer was homeless: sleeping in his car.
I am well aware that many of the homeless in America are veterans. But this was the first time I saw things working the opposite way.

We all have stereotypes of homeless people. As a matter of fact, the word "homeless" is itself a stereotype. We see them as dirty, lazy, with no ambition, addicts, mentally ill, or criminals. Women make up 23% of all homeless people, children are another 8%. Let me say that again: 8% of homeless are CHILDREN! Only 17.8% are chronically homeless. (Stats per the latest HUD report to Congress, 2013.) The vast majority are people just like you and me who are recovering from life altering events such as a lost job, family breakup, emergency or health crisis that took away their livelihood. There but by the grace of God, go you or me.

We were at Marine Corp Air Station Miramar for the annual "Relationship, Parenting & Marriage Expo". Hundreds of Marines and Sailors and their families passed our booth. We were there to share with them Christ Ministry Center's "Fount of Blessings" project (MyFOUNT.com) to which Tom was referring. It is a website we have been working on for two years making available a way to find information about the abundant "Streams of Mercy" (food, clothing, shelter, counseling, and two dozen other services) being offered by churches, charities, social services and government agencies. Anyone can use MyFOUNT.com free of charge! It's like Google in that anyone can search for hundreds of services being offered right in their own city or neighborhood.

There is perhaps no better way for churches, charities and social agencies to become more efficient and effective in meeting the needs of the homeless, hungry, hurting and hopeless than through The Fount. It truly is a revolutionary new way for us all to collaborate in meeting needs, especially as governments cut social programs. Who knows? Maybe the person living out of their car today might just be the person who saves your way of life once they get back on their feet. Here is the background on The Fount.

Chapter 28: The Exodus Story
(Coming Full Circle)

"You don't have to wait for the End. I am, right now, Resurrection and Life. The one who believes in me, even though he or she dies, will live. And everyone who lives believing in me does not ultimately die at all. Do you believe this?" (John 11:25-26)

Exodus Baptist Church came to Christ United Methodist in February 2005 seeking a place to worship. Since their inception in Pastor Owens' living room in June 2003, they had been meeting at first as a home church and then in a Masonic Lodge. They had grown to the point where they needed to worship and serve from a church. After giving notice to end their lease, Exodus began at Easter 2005 conducting services in our sanctuary on Sundays at 9:00 a.m.

God had impressed upon me the concept of the Ministry Center for over a year before Exodus arrived. But it was in May 2005 that I finally shared the concept with Christ Church.

So it was at the same time I shared the Ministry Center concept that Exodus Baptist Church came to us seeking a home. Was this a coincidence? I think not! Exodus Church has been a part of God's plan for Christ Ministry Center from the beginning.

From the first moment, Pastor Donald Owens and I connected spiritually. We have been the best of friends for over a decade. We conducted joint worship services at Easter, Pentecost and Christmas, and worked together on the annual Community Thanksgiving Meal and Children's Easter Festival. The bond would be enduring. We became a family!

Operation Baby Buggy
It was only a few months after we met, that Hurricane Katrina devastated the Gulf Coast. Pastor Owens was a native of Louisiana, and I was from Mississippi. We wanted to do what we could to help. We decided to fill an 18-wheeler full of baby supplies and send it to the Gulf Coast. "Project Baby Buggy" was the first truck to cross the state line into Mississippi near Slidell with much needed relief for the storm's most vulnerable victims. This was the first of many joint projects between Exodus and Christ UMC.

It has taken a decade for both Exodus and CMC to come full circle. On February 15, 2015, almost exactly a decade to the day Exodus first walked

through our doors, Bishop Minerva Carcaño held a Constituting
Conference for Exodus *United Methodist* Church.

A Resurrection Story and Grand Experiment

Bishop Carcaño called this "A resurrection story." Out of the passing of
Christ United Methodist Church, Exodus United Methodist Church was
born.

Christ UMC closed in July 2011, and Christ Ministry Center immediately
assumed the charter to operate as an urban Ministry Center using the
facilities of old Christ Church. It was a grand experiment, for there was no
clearly defined plan in The Book of Discipline for creating and operating a
"Ministry Center".

In 2005, Christ Church shared space with four congregations. In addition
to Christ Church and Exodus, Ministerio Hispano of San Diego was under
the leadership of Rev. Guillermo Prince, a retired Methodist pastor from
Mexico. In 2009, a group of Haitian refugees sought asylum in San Diego
and began worshipping at Christ UMC. All four groups had strong
Wesleyan roots. But no one of the congregations was strong enough to
assume responsibility for the financial and maintenance requirements
needed to continue operating as a church.

A Brief Separation

It was a sad day in June 2010 when I learned Exodus Baptist Church was
moving out of Christ Church because they had an opportunity to purchase
their own church building. Like a parent whose child leaves home for
college, there were mixed feelings. It is only natural that a growing church
should want to have its own building. But we maintained close ties. I was
honored to be invited to preach at the Exodus Church Ninth Anniversary in
2012. But for whatever reason, the new building situation did not work out.

Pastor Owens and I continued to meet for lunch on a regular basis. I even
offered to help Exodus work out financing to purchase a church that had
closed. As we talked, I invited Exodus Baptist back to Christ Ministry
Center. Exodus returned "home" to CMC in October 2012.

Exodus Baptist becomes Exodus Methodist

It was then Pastor Owens shared that God was leading him to consider
becoming United Methodist, and perhaps the entire Exodus congregation
would become United Methodist too!

Having made the transition from Baptist to Methodist in my own personal life, I knew this was not a decision to be made quickly. We agreed that we would take a year in which Pastor Owens and I would explore the history, doctrine and polity of the United Methodist Church. If at the end of that year he was still convinced God was leading in this direction, we would take yet another year, to educate the congregation on the ramifications of becoming Methodist. Only then would we petition the California Pacific Annual Conference for a charter for Exodus UMC.

A Modern Pentecost

Not only was this an unusual arrangement in that Christ Ministry Center and Exodus UMC would both hold charters and operate from the building, but the nature of the church itself was not the norm.

Exodus UMC was predominately African-American. Ministerio Hispano was of course Hispanic/Latino. The Haitian congregation was Haitian and spoke Creole. And the legacy Christ UMC congregation, now called Christ Chapel, was a small but ethnically mixed congregation of mostly Anglo-Americans.

It took over a year for the Cabinet and Bishop to approve creation of Exodus UMC. Because Pastor Owens had not had time to become an elder, the Bishop agreed to charter Exodus if I would come out of retirement and serve as "Pastor in Charge". Since I was Director of the Ministry Center and at the church almost every day, the additional responsibilities were not unmanageable. Pastor Owens handled pulpit responsibilities and pastoral care while I oversaw that Exodus became trained and organized according to the Book of Discipline. My duties included overseeing the ministry team consisting of Pastor Owens, and three ethnic-language lay ministers.

Exodus UMC is as close to the experience of Pentecost in Acts as I have ever witnessed. We are in one place holding all things in one accord. The styles of worship and languages differ, but the beauty of holiness emerges when we combine as one family.

God Did It Again

When Exodus left Christ United Methodist in 2010, I had never imagined that they would return to Meade and 33rd Street, much less become United Methodists! Exodus Church has always been deeply involved in street ministries and we shared a common goal of helping the helpless. This was an opportunity for us to strengthen each other through our shared passions. Little did I know God was at work providing "Centergy" between CMC and Exodus Church.

179

Our three small struggling ministries (Hispanic, Haitian and the legacy Christ Chapel) were immediately strengthened and blessed when they united with Exodus Church. What neither one could do alone, we were able to do together. Everyone involved benefited. God continues to bless us.

Chapter 29: "The Miracle on 33rd Street"
(Succeeding)

"This Temple is going to end up far better than it started out, a glorious beginning but an even more glorious finish: a place in which I will hand out wholeness and holiness." (Haggai 2:9)

Imagine for a moment a Sunday morning worship service at Old First Church with 40 gray-haired members seated in a sanctuary designed to hold 400. The median age of those members is 72. Three-fourths are women, mostly widows. Over half are barely surviving on Social Security.

They love the Lord and they love their old church. The roof leaks when it rains. The insurance and utilities have doubled over the last few years. None of them want to face the reality that they do not have the energy, manpower or resources to maintain the building, much less operate a food pantry or clothes closet. Thank God the pastor is retired, but continues to serve on his modest pension.

They are holding on, hoping for a miracle.

Now imagine the scene a year later. Two dozen middle age adults are setting up the Social Hall for the Friday grocery distribution. A hundred high school students and faculty attend the alternative high school that meets in the basement. Thirty or more neighbors start their weekday support group at the church they would never otherwise have attended. Over 1,200 people come in contact with the church or one of its ministries every week.

The leaky roof has been fixed and paid for. The hallways, bathrooms and social hall sport a new coat of paint.

What happened? The miracle did indeed come about, but it didn't look like the miracle they prayed for. The legacy congregation decided to move from a dying church on the chopping block, to become a Ministry Center.

Miracles on 33rd Street
Because we are located at the corner of Meade Avenue and 33rd Street, it is our own "Miracle on 33rd Street".

In retrospect, I have seen many "Miracles on 33rd Street":

- That Christ Church would close, but give birth to Christ Ministry Center.
- That Christ Ministry Center would be completely self-supporting from the first day.
- That our under-utilized old building would see every available space used every week, if not every day, in some form of ministry.
- That over 1,200 people would be touched every week by at least one of the ministries at CMC.
- That Exodus Church would come along side to support us.
- That combined with our Haitian, Hispanic and Christ Chapel ministries, Exodus United Methodist Church would become the first new UMC church in San Diego in decades!
- That The Fount of Blessings would extend from CMC into all 50 states.

How likely were any of these things, and dozens more, miracles to occur? Each of these were stepping stones in God's plan for CMC. The future looks bright for Christ Ministry Center and Exodus United Methodist Church as we continue to fulfill our mission.

Our Ministry Center family of churches and charities is an ever-changing kaleidoscope as charities lose grants and close, as churches outgrow us, and as new congregations and nonprofits arrive seeking a home. Today, we have more churches, charities and social agencies than we had active members at closure. Here is a snapshot (November 2015):

Churches, Charities and Ministries at Christ Ministry Center

PARTNERS
AngelCare (Child Sponsors)
Brother's Keeper Clothes Closet (Open Monday-Friday 8:00-3:30)
Crossroads Christian Ministry (Grocery distribution Tuesdays and Fridays)
Dress for Success San Diego (Clothes closet for women's apparel and career assistance)
Exodus Food Pantry (Open Monday-Friday 8:00-3:30)
Family Health Centers of San Diego (Satellite for health and health insurance for underserved populations)
Gambling Recovery Ministries (West Coast headquarters for GRM)
Goodwill Industries – Job Fair and Career Development
Here and Now (NA support group, meets M-F 9:00-10:00)
Jubilee Economic Ministries (Economic and Ecological Justice)

Juvenile Court and Community School (approximately 100 students and staff meet M-F 8:00-4:00, run jointly by Juvenile Court and SD County Office of Education)

LifeLine Screening (Periodic health screenings - usually quarterly)

Monday Night AA Group (Closed men's group, meets Mondays 7:00-9:00 pm)

Toys for Tots

Union of Pan American Communities (MOU for Adult and Adolescent Alcohol Treatment and Recovery)

Waters of Jordan Enrichment Center (ministry for abused women and children at risk)

Welcome Home Ministries (MOU Women's Prison and Re-entry Ministry - "First Stop" for Las Colinas)

ALLIANCES
SD Alliance - Immigrant Rights Consortium
SD Reentry Roundtable
SD Region Interfaith Coalition

CHURCHES
Be Encouraged in the Word Church
Bethel Seventh Day Adventist Church
Boulevard Abbey Anglican Church
Eritrean Christian Church
Ethiopian Orthodox Church
Exodus United Methodist Church (African-American, Haitian, Hispanic and legacy Anglo ministries)
New Jerusalem Church
SD Marshallese Church (United Church of Christ)

And, of course, THE FOUNT OF BLESSINGS (MyFOUNT.com)

This is the story of what happened at Christ Ministry Center in San Diego. We hope that in sharing our story we may provide a model for any church facing closure, as well as inspiration, hope and a blueprint for your own miracle.

Chapter 30: Epilogue
"Officially closed, but open to new ministry"

The following is an article written by Linda Bloom, United Methodist News Service journalist in New York that appeared August 27, 2014 on www.umc.org.

Eight years ago, when it seemed inevitable that Christ United Methodist Church in San Diego would eventually close, the Rev. Bill Jenkins convinced his dwindling congregation to take a slightly different path.

In the process, the congregation offered a home to a dozen multi-ethnic congregations of various faiths and space to social programs serving their North Park neighborhood while saving a historic building.

When it was constructed in the 1950s, what was then the First Evangelical United Brethren Church of San Diego housed the largest EUB congregation west of the Rocky Mountains. The Evangelical United Brethren and Methodist denominations merged to form the United Methodist Church in 1968.

As with many urban churches, times had changed at Christ church. "Here was a church that was used one hour on a Sunday morning," explained Jenkins, who became pastor there in 1999. "Some of those rooms had not been used in decades."

Today, the doors at the 25,000-square-foot Christ United Methodist Ministry Center open at 8 a.m. daily and don't close again until 9:30 or 10 p.m., touching some 1,000 lives a week, he estimated. "It was just amazing the people God brought to us," the 66-year-old pastor said.

The transformation came with the support of the United Methodist California-Pacific Annual (regional) Conference. "Like a lot of urban congregations, its core members were mostly commuting from other places," recalled the Rev. Myron Wingfield, who was the South District superintendent at the time and now is on staff at the United Methodist Board of Higher Education and Ministry in Nashville, Tennessee.

What made the project work were good collaborative choices, Wingfield added. Church members were willing to start meeting the needs of the community, with Jenkins providing the leadership.

"It's an uncommon collection of factors that really has led to a vital presence of ministry in that location," he added.

Trajectory toward social justice
Perhaps the most important factor is Jenkins himself, who stayed on the center's executive director. Like the church, he has been on a lifelong journey of transformation and faith.

As a teenager living in segregated Yazoo City, Mississippi, in the 1960s, Jenkins found his white friends were more interested in the 100th anniversary of the Civil War than the passage of the Civil Rights Act.

But he had a different perspective, he said, gained from the summers he spent helping his father with a dry cleaning route in the Delta, where 90 percent of the clients were black sharecroppers. As a Delta State University student, he broke the color barrier at an all-black high school when he took a student teaching position there.

The two experiences, Jenkins explained, "set my life in a whole different trajectory."

His life in the ministry began with ordination in the Southern Baptist Church at the age of 20. The ideological shift in the Southern Baptist Convention after 1978 was troubling to Jenkins and when he joined The United Methodist Church in 1988, "I knew that I was home," he recalled.

Wingfield credits the "tri-vocational" experience that Jenkins gained over the years — in education and technology as well as the ministry — "combined with a very passionate faith and guided by a generous willingness to truly be the church" with making the project sustainable.

"The diversity of the community brought together there is also a key piece," Wingfield said, adding that Jenkins' willingness to open the space to congregations of other denominations and develop a relationship with their leaders and key members was in "the Catholic spirit" espoused by John Wesley, the founder of Methodism.

Fostering diversity
A prime example is the Haitian gospel music group, "Louange a Dieu" – Creole for "Praises to God." Jenkins befriended the group in 2009 after he learned gangs in Haiti were persecuting them.

Jenkins made the chapel available to the group on Sunday evenings, but the help didn't stop there. "We converted space in the church so they could live, sleep, cook and shower in the huge building," he explained. Then he searched for "the best immigration attorney I could find."

After a massive earthquake struck Haiti on Jan. 12, 2010, the now-established Haitian Methodist congregation became "the hub" of relief efforts in San Diego, Jenkins said.

When Haitians refugees began to reach the U.S. border through Mexico, U.S. Immigration and Custom Enforcement officers turned to the congregation and Christ Church for help and translation services. With assistance from the United Methodist Committee on Relief and Catholic Charities of San Diego, former Sunday school rooms in the education building were transformed into temporary housing for more than 300 Haitian refugees.

The granting of temporary protected status to Haitians who were in the United States before the earthquake "was a game changer for them," Jenkins said about the Haitian congregation. "They were able to get jobs, such as orderlies and custodians at the hospital and nursing homes. Most enrolled in extension courses to pick up marketable skills."

Jenkins said he is humbled and proud to be called "father" by the Haitian group. "I consider the Haitians my children, especially the original Louange a Dieu group," he explained. "They are young adults, and we have been through so much together."

Death leads to resurrection
Realizing that the original Christ United Methodist Church was no longer sustainable in a traditional sense, the South District, which includes San Diego, and then Bishop Mary Ann Swenson were willing "to name that and embrace a certain type of death with hope of resurrection," Wingfield said.

The church was de-commissioned in 2011 — although Christ Chapel, a small United Methodist group, still worships there — and the ministry center emerged. As a retired elder, Jenkins could still serve the sacraments and provide denominational oversight.

Admittedly, for a period of time after the transition, Christ Ministry Center "kind of fell off the radar" for the conference, said the Rev. John Farley,

Wingfield's successor as district superintendent. "Bill was there just keeping things going without any official capacity."

Farley said he admires the way Jenkins has claimed the history of change, renewal and rebirth in an older neighborhood that is ethnically diverse and becoming popular with young families.

"Bill's kind of an entrepreneurial spirit and a great evangelical spirit at the same time," he said.

What's most exciting to Farley is the connection that is growing among four of the faith groups meeting at the ministry center who together average 220 in worship. "The story we say is they fell in love with each other," he explained. "They began to feel like a unique family. Organically, this diversity began to sort of merge."

The groups have been studying Methodist theology and are considering a constituting conference to become a new United Methodist congregation. "They're finding a home in Wesleyan grace," Farley said.

Bloom is a United Methodist News Service multimedia reporter based in New York.

SECTION SIX: Appendices

Appendix A: Typical Church Business Model

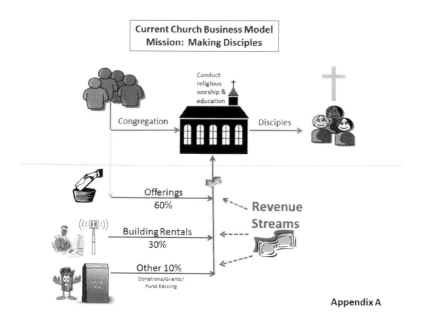

Appendix A

Appendix B: Ministry Center Business Model

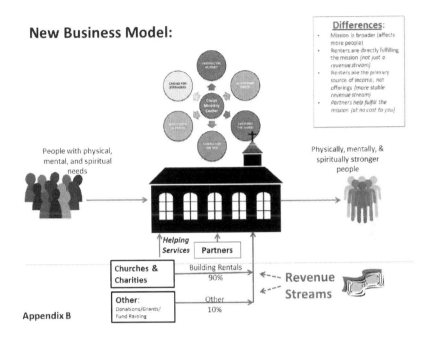

Appendix C: Resolution of Discontinuance

Daily Proceedings (pages D53-D54)
California-Pacific Annual Conference
June 16-19, 2011
Redlands, California

Christ UMC: San Diego: Rev. Myron Wingfield, San Diego District Superintendent presented a Resolution for Discontinuance of Christ United Methodist Church and a name change to Christ United Methodist Church Ministry Center. It was supported.

WHEREAS the Christ United Methodist Church located in San Diego County was founded by the merger of two congregations - First United Brethren in Christ of San Diego (founded 1908) and Emmanuel Church of the Evangelical Association (founded 1911) – in 1946 as First Evangelical United Brethren Church of San Diego, then became Christ United Methodist Church when the EUB and Methodist Church merged in 1968; and

WHEREAS all three congregations together represent a long and proud history of mission and ministry in San Diego; and

WHEREAS the building and grounds of Christ United Methodist Church have been, and continue to be, a vital outpost for mission and ministry by housing a variety of ministries that directly serve the surrounding neighborhood and the broader community of San Diego; and

WHEREAS the church conference of the Christ United Methodist Church voted on May 21, 2011 to discontinue the church; and

WHEREAS the district superintendent has recommended discontinuance of the Christ United Methodist Church and the retention of the remaining membership as a mission congregation of the San Diego District; and

WHEREAS the superintendent has recommended that all of the real and personal property of Christ United Methodist Church be held in trust by the mission congregation, in the same corporate entity as was formerly used by Christ United Methodist Church when it was a chartered local United Methodist Church, and utilized as Christ United Methodist Ministry Center; and

WHEREAS the consent to discontinue has been granted by the presiding bishop, a vote of the majority of the district superintendents, and the District Committee on Church Location and Building, and all proper *Disciplinary* requirements have been complied with;

THEREFORE, BE IT RESOLVED that the Christ United Methodist Church be discontinued effective on a date after July 1, 2011, that date to be determined by the District Superintendent; and

BE IT FURTHER RESOLVED that the site be designated as Christ United Methodist Ministry Center following the date of discontinuance.

Appendix D: Revenue and Cost Comparison

Current Revenues (Annual)				Anticipated Future Revenues (Annual)		
Source	Amount	Type		Source	Amount	Type
Offerings	$30,000	Continuing		Offerings	$0	Continuing
Cell Tower A	$30,000	Continuing		Cell Tower A	$30,000	Continuing
Cell Tower B	$25,000	Continuing		Cell Tower B	$25,000	Continuing
Cell Tower C	$30,000	Continuing		Cell Tower C	$30,000	Continuing
Grants	$25,000	Continuing		Grants	$10,000	One Time
Donations	$12,000	Continuing		Donations/Tithes	$5,000	Continuing
School rental	$60,000	Continuing		School rental	$60,000	Continuing
Fund Raisers	$10,000	One Time		Charity A Rental	$8,000	Continuing
				Charity B Rental	$6,000	Continuing
				Charity C Rental	$5,400	Continuing
				Charity D Rental	$4,800	Continuing
				Church A Rental	$24,000	Continuing
				Church B Rental	$18,000	Continuing
				Church C Rental	$9,000	Continuing
				Legacy Church	$5,000	Continuing
				Partners Revenue	$6,000	Continuing
TOTAL:	$220,000			TOTAL:	$246,200	

Current Costs (Annual)				Anticipated Future Costs (Annual)		
Source	Amount	Type		Source	Amount	Type
Utilities	$28,000	Continuing		Utilities	$32,000	Continuing
Maintenance	$48,000	Continuing		Maintenance	$52,000	Continuing
Administration	$6,300	Continuing		Administration	$6,500	Continuing
Insurance & Tax	$16,000	Continuing		Insurance & Tax	$18,000	Continuing
Personnel Costs	$120,000	Continuing		Personnel Costs	$100,000	Continuing
Debt Reduction	$6,000	Continuing		Debt Reduction	$6,000	Continuing
TOTAL:	$224,300			TOTAL:	$214,500	
Net Loss/YR	($2,300)			Net Gain/YR	$31,700	

Appendix E: By-Laws

ARTICLE 1: OFFICES

1.1 Principal Office. The location of the principal executive office of Christ United Methodist Ministry Center, a California non-profit corporation (the Corporation") is 3295 Meade Avenue, San Diego, California 92116. The board of trustees of the Corporation (the "Board") may change the location of the Corporation's principal executive office at any time. Any change in location shall be noted by the secretary of the corporation (the "Secretary") on these Bylaws opposite this Section, or this Section may be amended to state the new location. The Board may, at any time, establish branch or subordinate offices wherever the Corporation is qualified to do business.

ARTICLE II: PURPOSE

2.1 Purpose. The purpose of Corporation is to (1) provide a nurturing environment for worship, religious education and fellowship for religious congregations in the advancement of religion; and provide a base of operations for charitable and community 501(c)(3) organizations engaged in public benefit ministries; especially relief of the poor, distressed and underprivileged; and (2) create and maintain a mechanism to harness the resources of existing 501(c)(3) charities and churches in the San Diego area which enables them more efficiency and effectiveness in helping the helpless. As such, the Corporation does not engage directly in ministries to individuals, but supports churches and charities that provide services and ministries for the relief of the poor, distressed, and underprivileged in the San Diego area.

2.2 Authority. The Trustees and Officers of the Corporation shall have the authority to act in service of the Corporation's purpose as outlined in Section 2.1.

ARTICLE III: TRUSTEES

3.1 Number of Trustees. The Directors of this Corporation shall be referred to as Trustees and shall have the same powers authorized to directors under applicable law. The authorized number of Trustees of the Corporation (each, a "Trustee" and, collectively, the "Trustees") shall be no less than six (6) and no more than nine (9), the exact number to be determined by the Board. For purposes of these Bylaws, "Authorized Number of Trustees" shall mean such exact number determined by the Board. Such minimum and maximum numbers may be changed only by an amendment of this Section approved by the Trustees consistent with the Corporation's

Conflict of Interest Policy attached hereto as Exhibit A and incorporated by reference (the "Conflict of Interest Policy").

3.2 Qualifications of Trustees. Each Trustee must meet the following qualifications: (a) Such Trustee must have previously served as a volunteer in a position of considerable responsibility in the Corporation or another religious or charitable entity and must demonstrate a commitment to serve the Corporation; (b) Such Trustee must agree to serve on the Board without remuneration; (c) Such Trustee must read, acknowledge and adhere to the Corporation's Conflict of Interest Policy at all times; and (d) No person may serve as a Trustee for more than 9 consecutive years (and any time spent as an officer of the Corporation shall not be considered in the calculation of such time period).

Powers of the Board. The Board shall have all the powers and privileges granted to directors of nonprofit corporations by the laws of the State of California.

3.3 Initial Trustees. The nine (9) Trustees appointed by the president of the Corporation (the "President") shall serve for up to three consecutive one year terms as determined at their time of appointment. The Board shall be broken up into three "Classes" consisting of three Trustees each. Only one Class shall rotate off every year so there is continuity on the Board. For illustration purposes, of the nine Trustees selected in 2013, a Class of three will be scheduled to rotate off in 2014 (subject to such Trustee's potential reelection), another Class of three will rotate off in 2015 and the last Class of three in 2016.

3.4 Nomination and Election of Trustees. At least 45 days prior to each annual Board meeting, the President shall appoint a Nominating Committee, consisting of only disinterested Trustees, meaning the Trustees not running for reelection during that term, for the purpose of nominating the Trustees to be elected for the following term. The President shall designate one of the Trustees on such Nominating Committee to be Chairperson of such Nominating Committee. Such Chairperson shall send a report to the Secretary at least 30 days prior to such upcoming annual Board meeting, notifying the Board of the slate of nominees for Trustees determined by such Nominating Committee. Such slate shall include at least the Authorized Number of Trustees, and may include such additional nominees as determined by such Nominating Committee. Additional nominations may also be made in accordance with the California Corporations Code. Trustees shall be elected to hold office for at least one year and up to a three-year period. Each Trustee, including a Trustee elected to fill a vacancy, shall hold office until the expiration of the term for which elected and until a successor has been elected.

3.6 Resignation and Removal of Trustees. Any Trustee may resign at any time by giving written notice to the President, the Secretary or the Board. Such resignation shall be effective upon giving such notice or at such later time specified in such notice. The Board may remove a Trustee for cause if (1) such Trustee is incapacitated and can no longer effectively render his or her duties; (2) such Trustee, in the Board's sole and absolute discretion, takes any action to harm the interests of the Corporation, including without limitation, engaging in an act in contravention of the Conflict of Interest Policy; (3) such Trustee is convicted of a felony. Any Trustee may be removed, with or without cause, if such removal is approved by a majority vote of disinterested Trustees. Any reduction of the Authorized Number of Trustees does not remove any Trustee prior to the expiration of such Trustee's term of office.

3.7 Filling Trustee Vacancies. Vacancies on the Board may be filled by a majority of the Trustees then in office, whether or not less than a quorum, or by a sole remaining Trustee, and each Trustee so elected shall hold office for the unexpired term of such Trustee's predecessor and until such Trustee's successor is elected at the next annual Board meeting.

3.8 Board Meetings. Board meetings shall be held at the principal executive office of the Corporation unless another place is stated in the notice of the meeting. A regular Board meeting shall be held annually at such place and time as may be determined by the President. Regular Board meetings shall also be held at least quarterly, at such place and time as may be determined by the President. Additional regular Board meetings shall be held, if so provided in a resolution adopted by the Board, at the time and place specified in such resolution. A special Board meeting may be called by the President or any four Trustees. Notice of all regular and special Board meetings shall be given in writing and emailed at least four days before the meeting or shall be delivered personally or by telephone at least two days before the meeting. Such notice need not be given any Trustee who signs a waiver of notice, whether before or after the meeting, or who attends the meeting without protesting, prior thereto, or at its commencement, the lack of notice to such Trustee. Such notice need not include the purpose or agenda for the meeting. Members of the Board may participate in a Board meeting through use of conference telephone or similar communications equipment, provided all Trustees participating in such Board meeting can hear one another. Participation in a Board meeting by such means constitutes presence in person at such Board meeting. A majority of the Authorized Number of Trustees constitutes a quorum of the Board for the transaction of business. A majority of the Trustees present, whether or not a quorum is present, may adjourn any Board meeting to another time and place. If the Board meeting is adjourned for more than two days, notice of any adjournment to another time or place shall be given, prior to the time of the adjourned Board meeting, to the Trustees who were not present at the time of the adjournment.

3.9 Required Vote of Trustees. Every act or decision done or made by a majority of the Trustees present at a Board meeting duly held at which a quorum is present is the act of the Board. A Board meeting at which a quorum is initially present may continue to transact business notwithstanding the withdrawal of Trustees, if any action taken is approved by at least a majority of the required quorum for such Board meeting.

3.10 Written Consent of Trustees. Any action required or permitted to be taken by the Board may be taken without a Board meeting, if all Trustees consent in writing to such action. Such written consent or consents shall be filed with the minutes of the proceedings of the Board. Such action by written consent shall have the same force and effect as a unanimous vote of such Trustees.

3.11 Committees with Legal Authority. The Board may, by resolution adopted by a majority of the Authorized Number of Trustees, appoint one or more committees with legal authority to act for the Corporation to the extent specified in such resolution, each such committee consisting of two or more Trustees, to serve at the pleasure of the Board. The Board may designate one or more Trustees as alternate members of any committee, who may replace any absent member at any meeting of such committee. The Sections above entitled "Board Meetings," "Required Vote of Trustees," and "Written Consent of Trustees," with appropriate adaptations to the circumstances, apply to the procedures of such committees (including without limitation the Nominating Committee set forth above). Any such committee, to the extent provided in the Board resolution appointing such committee, shall have the same authority as the Board, except with respect to (a) the filling of vacancies on the Board or on any committee, (b) the fixing of compensation for any person or company in service of the Corporation, (c) the amendment or repeal of these Bylaws or the adoption of new bylaws, (d) the amendment or repeal of any resolution of the Board which by its express terms may not be so amended or repealed, or (e) the appointment of other committees.

3.12 Advisory Committees. The Board may appoint advisory committees to consist of one or more individuals. Advisory committees may consist of Trustees, non-Trustees, and members of the public. Advisory committees have no legal authority to act for the Corporation, but shall report their findings and recommendations to the Board. The Board may authorize the implementation of any recommendation of such Committees, including the execution of any such recommendation by members of such Committees.

3.13 Fees and Compensation; Inspection Rights. Trustees and members of advisory committees shall not receive any reimbursement for expenses or compensation unless approved by a Board resolution. Any Trustee may at any reasonable time and upon reasonable notice, inspect and copy any books, records and documents of the Corporation and may inspect the physical properties of the Corporation. Such inspection may be made in person or by agent or attorney.

ARTICLE IV: OFFICERS

4.1 Officers and Duties. The officers of the Corporation are the President, the Secretary, the Chief Financial Officer, and such other officers as the Board may by resolution authorize:

4.1.1 President. The President shall preside at all Board meetings. The President shall, subject to the control of the Board, direct and control the business and affairs of the Corporation and of its officers, employees and agents. The President shall generally perform all the duties usually pertaining to the office.

4.1.2 Vice President. The Board may by resolution authorize one or more vice presidents to perform, under the direction of the President, duties and responsibilities in the management of the Corporation or in particular areas of its management. If the President becomes disabled, then the duties of the President
shall be exercised by any person designated by the Board, or in the absence of such designation, by the senior vice president of the Corporation, if one exists.

4.1.3 Secretary. The Secretary shall keep (or cause to be kept) the minute book of the Corporation. The Secretary shall sign in the name of the Corporation, either alone or with one or more other officers, all documents authorized or required to be signed by the Secretary. If the Corporation has a corporate seal, the Secretary shall keep the seal and shall affix the seal to documents as appropriate or desired. The Board may by resolution authorize one or more assistant secretaries to perform, under the direction of the Secretary, some or all of the duties of the Secretary.

4.1.4 Chief Financial Officer. The Chief Financial Officer is responsible for the receipt, maintenance and disbursement of the Corporation's funds. The Chief Financial Officer shall keep (or cause to be kept) books and records of account and records of all properties of the Corporation. The Chief Financial Officer shall prepare (or cause to be prepared) annually, or more often if so directed by the Board or the President, financial statements of the Corporation. The Chief Financial Officer shall be deemed to be the treasurer of the Corporation for purposes of giving any reports or executing any documents or instruments requiring the signature of the "treasurer." The Board may by resolution authorize one or more assistant financial officers to perform, under the direction of the Chief Financial Officer, some or all of the duties of the Chief Financial Officer.

4.2 Election and Removal of Officers. The President, the Secretary and the Chief Financial Officer shall be elected by the Board. Other officers shall be elected or appointed as prescribed in the Board resolution authorizing such officer. Any officer may be removed from office at any time by the Board, with or without cause or prior notice. When authorized by the Board, any officer may be elected for a specified term under a contract of employment. Notwithstanding that such officer is elected for a specified term or under a contract of employment, any such officer may be removed from office at any time pursuant to this Section and shall have no claim against the Corporation on account of such removal other than for such monetary compensation as such officer may be entitled to under the terms of the contract of employment. Any officer may resign at any time upon written notice to the Corporation without prejudice to the rights, if any, of the Corporation under any contract to which the officer is a party. Such resignation shall be effective upon giving such notice or at such later time specified in such notice.

ARTICLE V: INDEMNIFICATION

5.1 Indemnification. The Corporation shall, to the maximum extent permitted by California Corporations Code Section 5238, indemnify each person against all expenses, judgments, fines, settlements and other amounts actually and reasonably incurred in connection with any proceeding arising from the fact that such person is or was an agent of the

Corporation if such person acted in good faith and in a manner such person reasonably believed to be in the best interests of the Corporation and, in the case of a criminal proceeding, had no reasonable cause to believe the conduct of such person was unlawful. For the purposes of this Section, an "agent" of the Corporation includes a person who is or was a Trustee, officer, employee, or other agent of the Corporation, or is or was serving at the request of the Corporation as a director, officer, employee, or agent of another corporation, partnership, joint venture, trust or other enterprise.

ARTICLE VI: MEMBERS

6.1 Membership. The Corporation shall have no members.

ARTICLE VII: RECORDS

7.1 Minute Book. The Corporation shall keep a minute book which shall contain the following:

7.1.1 The record of all Board meetings including date, place, those attending and the proceedings thereof, a copy of the notice of meeting and when and how given, written waivers of notice of meeting, written consents to holding meeting, written approvals of minutes of meeting, and unanimous written consents to action of the Board without a meeting, and similarly as to meetings of committees of the Board.

7.1.2 A copy of the articles of incorporation and all amendments thereto and a copy of all certificates filed with the California Secretary of State.

7.1.3 A copy of the bylaws as amended, duly certified by the Secretary.

ARTICLE VII: AMENDMENT OF BYLAWS

8.1 Amendment. Except as provided in the Section above entitled "Number of Trustees," these Bylaws may be amended or repealed either by approval of at least 60 percent of the Authorized Number of Trustees.

CERTIFICATE OF SECRETARY

The undersigned hereby certifies as follows:

1. The undersigned is the presently elected and acting secretary of Christ United Methodist Ministry Center, a California public benefit corporation.

2. These Bylaws consisting of 7 pages, are the bylaws of such corporation as ratified by its Board of Trustees effective November __, 2013.

Dated: _____, 2013

By: _____
      Corporate Secretary

Appendix F: Conflict of Interest Policy

ARTICLE I
Purpose

The purpose of the conflict of interest policy is to protect the interest of Christ United Methodist Ministry Center, non-profit organization (hereinafter, the "Organization") when it is contemplating entering into a transaction or arrangement that might benefit the private interest of an officer or Trustee of the Organization or might result in a possible excess benefit transaction.

This policy is intended to supplement but not replace any applicable state and federal laws governing conflict of interest applicable to the Organization or other nonprofit and charitable organizations.

ARTICLE II
Definitions

"Interested Person": Any Trustee, principal officer, or member of a committee with Board delegated powers, who has a direct or indirect Financial Interest, as defined below, is an Interested Person.

"Financial Interest": A person has a Financial Interest if the person has, directly or indirectly, through business, investment, or family:

An ownership or investment interest in any entity with which the Organization has a transaction or arrangement;

A compensation arrangement with the Organization or with any entity or individual with which the Organization has a transaction or arrangement, or;

A potential ownership or investment interest in, or compensation arrangement with, any entity or individual with which the Organization is negotiating a transaction or arrangement. Compensation includes direct and indirect remuneration as well as gifts or favors that are not insubstantial.

A Financial Interest is not necessarily a conflict of interest. Under Article III, Section 2, a person who has a Financial Interest may have a conflict of interest only if the appropriate Board or committee decides that a conflict of interest exists.

ARTICLE III
Procedures

Duty to Disclose. In connection with any actual or possible conflict of interest, an Interested Person must disclose the existence of the Financial Interest and be given the opportunity to disclose all material facts to the Trustees and members of committees with Board of Trustees ("Board") delegated powers considering the proposed transaction or arrangement.

Determining Whether a Conflict of Interest Exists. After disclosure of the Financial Interest and all material facts, and after any discussion with the Interested Person, he/she shall leave the Board or committee meeting while the determination of a conflict of interest is discussed and voted upon. The remaining Board or committee members shall decide if a conflict of interest exists.

Procedures for Addressing the Conflict of Interest. An Interested Person may make a presentation at the Board or committee meeting, but after the presentation, he/she shall leave the meeting during the discussion of, and the vote on, the transaction or arrangement involving the possible conflict of interest.

The chairperson of the Board or committee shall, if appropriate, appoint a disinterested person or committee to investigate alternatives to the proposed transaction or arrangement.

After exercising due diligence, the Board or committee shall determine whether the Organization can obtain with reasonable efforts a more advantageous transaction or arrangement from a person or entity that would not give rise to a conflict of interest.

If a more advantageous transaction or arrangement is not reasonably possible under circumstances not producing a conflict of interest, the Board or committee shall determine by a majority vote of the disinterested Trustees whether the transaction or arrangement is in the Organization's best interest, for its own benefit, and whether it is fair and reasonable. In conformity with the above determination it shall make its decision as to whether to enter into the transaction or arrangement.

\Violations of the Conflicts of Interest Policy. If the Board or committee has reasonable cause to believe a member has failed to disclose actual or possible conflicts of interest, it shall inform the member of the basis for such belief and afford the member an opportunity to explain the alleged failure to disclose.

If, after hearing the member's response and after making further investigation as warranted by the circumstances, the Board or committee determines the member has failed to disclose an actual or possible conflict of interest, it shall take appropriate disciplinary and corrective action.

ARTICLE IV
Records of Proceedings

The minutes of the Board and all committees with board delegated powers shall contain:
The names of the persons who disclosed or otherwise were found to have a Financial Interest in connection with an actual or possible conflict of interest, the nature of the Financial Interest, any action taken to determine whether a conflict of interest was present, and the Board's or committee's decision as to whether a conflict of interest in fact existed.

The names of the persons who were present for discussions and votes relating to the transaction or arrangement, the content of the discussion, including any alternatives to the proposed transaction or arrangement, and a record of any votes taken in connection with the proceedings.

ARTICLE V
Compensation

A voting member of the Board who receives compensation, directly or indirectly, from the Organization for services is precluded from voting on matters pertaining to that member's compensation.

A voting member of any committee whose jurisdiction includes compensation matters and who receives compensation, directly or indirectly, from the Organization for services is precluded from voting on matters pertaining to that member's compensation.

No voting member of the Board or any committee whose jurisdiction includes compensation matters and who receives compensation, directly or indirectly, from the Organization, either individually or collectively, is prohibited from providing information to any committee regarding compensation.

ARTICLE VI
Annual Statements

Each Trustee, principal officer and member of a committee with Board delegated powers shall annually sign a statement which affirms such person:

Has received a copy of this Conflict of Interest Policy, (the "Policy");

Has read and understands the Policy;

Has agreed to comply with the Policy; and

Understands the Organization is charitable and in order to maintain its federal tax exemption it must engage primarily in activities which accomplish one or more of its tax-exempt purposes.

ARTICLE VII
Periodic Reviews

To ensure the Organization operates in a manner consistent with charitable purposes and does not engage in activities that could jeopardize its tax-exempt status, periodic reviews shall be conducted. The periodic reviews shall, at a minimum, include the following subjects:

Whether compensation arrangements and benefits are reasonable, based on competent survey information, and the result of arm's length bargaining.

Whether partnerships, joint ventures, and arrangements with management organizations conform to the Organization's written policies, are properly recorded, reflect reasonable investment or payments for goods and services, further charitable purposes and do not result in inurement, impermissible private benefit or in an excess benefit transaction.

ARTICLE VIII
Use of Outside Experts

When conducting the periodic reviews as provided for in Article VII, the Organization may, but need not, use outside advisors. If outside experts are used, their use shall not relieve the Board of its responsibility for ensuring periodic reviews are conducted.

ACKNOWLEDGEMENT

I, _____, serving in the capacity of _____ for Christ United Methodist Ministry Center (the "Organization") acknowledge:

I have received a copy of the Organization's Conflict of Interest Policy (the "Policy");

I have read and understand the Policy,

I agree to comply with the Policy, and

I understand the Organization is charitable and in order to maintain its federal tax exemption it must engage primarily in activities which accomplish one or more of its tax-exempt purposes.

Date: _____   By: _____

Appendix G: Amendment of the Articles of Incorporation

The undersigned certify that:

They are the president and the secretary, respectively, of CHRIST UNITED METHODIST CHURCH OF SAN DIEGO, a California corporation.

The Articles of Incorporation as amended and restated on February 26, 1970 are hereby amended and restated to read as follows herein below.

This amendment of Articles of Incorporation has been duly approved by the Trustees which in this corporation act as its board of directors.

The corporation has no members.

ARTICLE I
The name of the Corporation shall be CHRIST UNITED METHODIST MINISTRY CENTER.

ARTICLE II
The corporation elects to be governed by all the provisions of the Nonprofit Corporation Law of 1980 not otherwise applicable to it under part 5 of division 2.

ARTICLE III
The corporation is a religious corporation and is not organized for the private gain of any person. It is organized under the Nonprofit Religious Corporation Law primarily for religious purposes.

The purpose of Christ United Methodist Ministry Center is to provide a nurturing environment for worship, education and fellowship for religious congregations and a base of operations for religious, charitable and community 501(c)(3) organizations engaged in public benefit ministries, especially: feeding the hungry, clothing the naked, befriending strangers, caring for captives, ministering to the sick, and quenching spiritual thirst.

ARTICLE IV
The corporation is organized for religious and charitable purposes within the meaning of Internal Revenue Code Section 501(c)(3). It shall not be operated, for pecuniary gain or profit, and it does not contemplate the distribution of gains, profits or dividends, to the members thereof or any

private shareholder or individual except that the corporation shall be authorized and empowered to pay reasonable compensation for services rendered and to make payments and distributions in furtherance of the purposes set forth in these articles.

The property, assets, profits and net income of this corporation are irrevocably dedicated to religious and charitable purposes, and no part of the profits or net income of this corporation shall ever inure to the benefit of any private person or individual.

Upon dissolution or winding up of this corporation, after paying or adequately providing for any debts or obligations of the corporation, the remaining assets shall be distributed to a nonprofit organization related to The United Methodist Church which is organized and operated exclusively for charitable or religious purposes and which has established its tax exempt status under Section 501(c)(3) and any subsequent applicable provisions of the Internal Revenue Code. If this corporation holds any assets on trust, such assets shall be disposed of in such a manner as may be directed by decree of the Superior Court of the County in which this corporation's principal office is located, upon petition therefor by the Attorney General, filed by any person concerned in the liquidation.

ARTICLE V

No substantial part of the activities of the corporation shall be the carrying on of propaganda, or otherwise attempting to influence legislation, and the corporation shall not participate in, or intervene in (including the publishing or distribution of statements) any political campaign on behalf of or in opposition to any candidate for public office. Notwithstanding any other provision of these articles, this corporation shall not, except to an insubstantial degree, engage in any activities or exercise any powers that are not in furtherance of the purposes of this corporation.

ARTICLE VI

The corporation shall have no voting members.

ARTICLE VII

The persons who are to act in the capacity of directors of this corporation shall be designated as trustees. The Board of Trustees shall be comprised of a minimum of six (6) and a maximum of nine (9) persons chosen in such a manner, time and place as shall be specified in the bylaws of the corporation.

That said trustees shall have the management and control of all the property of the corporation, subject to the provisions of the DISCIPLINE of the United Methodist Church and of the annual conference to which the ministry belongs, the bylaws adopted by the corporation consistent with said DISCIPLINE and the laws of the state or province by which the corporation is governed.

ARTICLE VIII

The Board of Trustees shall have the following officers: president, vice-president, secretary, and treasurer. The officers shall be selected annually by the Board of Trustees as specified in the bylaws of the corporation and shall perform the duties usually assigned to such officers. All vacancies occurring in the Board of Trustees shall be filled, and the business of the corporation shall be conducted in strict conformity with the bylaws of the corporation.

ARTICLE IX

The Board of Trustees shall hold an annual meeting before the last local conference in the fiscal year at which time the officers of the Board shall be elected. An annual report shall be prepared, including the transactions of the Board during the year and the condition of the property of the corporation, a copy of which shall be presented to the local conference. Special meetings of the Board and the corporation may be called by the president, or when requested by two (2) or more trustees.

ARTICLE X

All conveyances of property to this corporation shall be deeded in trust to be used, kept, maintained, and disposed of, for the use and benefit of the ministry and membership of the United Methodist Church. All real estate of the corporation, held in trust for the United Methodist Church, shall be sold and conveyed by the said trustees in the corporate name thereof, when the said trustees are authorized to do so by the corporation and the annual conference in whose bounds the corporation is situated.

ARTICLE XI

The corporation assumes to itself all the rights, powers, privileges and immunities which are now, and which, during the existence thereof, may be conferred by law upon corporations of a similar character.

We further declare under penalty of perjury under the laws of the State of California that the matters set forth in this certificate are true and correct of our own knowledge.

IN WITNESS WHEREOF, the undersigned have executed this Certificate of Amendment this _19th__ day of October, 2013.

_____

President of CHRIST UNITED METHODIST CHURCH OF SAN DIEGO

_____

Secretary of CHRIST UNITED METHODIST CHURCH OF SAN DIEGO

Appendix H: IRS Form 1023

PART IV: Narrative Description of Your Activities
PAST: Between 1911 and 1913, Emmanuel Evangelical and First United Brethren in Christ churches were formed in San Diego, California and maintained separate congregations. The two churches merged in 1946 to form First Evangelical United Brethren (EUB) Church of San Diego. In 1968, the Evangelical United Brethren and Methodist Church merged to form The United Methodist Church. In 1970, First EUB Church of San Diego changed its name to Christ United Methodist Church (CUMC).

In 2005, due to its inability to remain a traditional self-supporting church, CUMC began making plans to transition into the role of an urban ministry center that would share its large facilities with other congregations and convert their former classrooms into office space for churches and 501(c)(3) organizations.

PRESENT AND FUTURE: In June 2011, The United Methodist Church discontinued CUMC and created Christ United Methodist Ministry Center (CUMMC) as an organization exclusively supporting one or more charitable and religious organizations that are themselves classified as public charities under section 501(c)(3) of the Internal Revenue Code.

CUMMC is an ecumenical, non-profit faith-based urban ministry agency of The United Methodist Church. CUMMC is home to several congregations who share worship space. Various non-profit and charitable 501(c)(3) organizations, some with worldwide outreach, have offices at CUMMC.

PURPOSE: The purpose of Christ United Methodist Ministry Center is to (1) provide a nurturing environment for worship, religious education and fellowship for religious congregations in the advancement of religion; and provide a base of operations for charitable and community 501(c)(3) organizations engaged in public benefit ministries; especially relief of the poor, distressed and underprivileged; and (2) create and maintain a mechanism to harness the resources of existing 501(c)(3) charities and churches in the San Diego area which enables them more efficiency and effectiveness in helping the helpless.

As such, CUMMC does not engage directly in ministries to individuals, but supports churches and charities that provide services and ministries for the relief of the poor, distressed, and underprivileged in the San Diego area.

ACTIVITIES:
CUMMC's primary activity has been and will continue to be providing worship and religious education space for congregations without their own buildings, and providing office space in the San Diego area, for 501(c)(3) charities engaged in relief of the poor, distressed, and underprivileged. CUMMC's staff includes a director, office manager, custodian, sexton, and volunteer facilities person who manage the operations and maintenance of the facilities which requires approximately 70% of the staff's total time. The facilities are open from 7:30 a.m. to 9:30 p.m. weekdays, and 8:00 a.m. to 9:00 p.m. weekends. By providing these facilities, CUMMC furthers its exempt purposes by supporting the advancement of religion for otherwise homeless congregations. The activity is funded by each church or charity paying rental fees, and by donations, and grants.

CUMMC has developed an online database called Fount of Blessings that connects, publicizes, and promotes 501(c)(3) organizations in the San Diego area who are providing services to the poor, distressed and underprivileged, such as (but not limited to): feeding the hungry, clothing the naked, befriending strangers, caring for captives, ministering to the sick and quenching spiritual thirst. (See Fount brochure attached.) The CUMMC Director created, maintains, promotes, and raises funds for the database. The Office Manager and volunteers collect and input information into the database, collectively requiring 30% of the staff's total working time. The Fount database is available online 24 hours a day. The Fount furthers the exempt purpose of CUMMC by enabling these organizations to better support the poor, distressed and underprivileged populations they seek to serve. The Fount will be funded through a nominal use fee from participating 501(c)(3) organizations, and potential corporate sponsors, online donations, and grants.

PART VI: Your Members and Other Individuals and Organizations That Receive Benefits From You
The benefits CUMMC provides to those 501(c)(3) churches and charities that operate from our facilities include: office, religious education, kitchen, and meeting spaces; facilities maintenance; utilities; insurance; and some clerical/receptionist services by the office manager.

The benefits CUMMC provides to organizations through the Fount of Blessings program include an online database that connects, publicizes, and promotes 501(c)(3) organizations in the San Diego area who are providing services to the poor, distressed and underprivileged. The Fount offers a resource for connecting volunteers to these organizations.

PART VIII: Your Specific Activities
We do not attempt to influence legislation.

PART VIII.15: Do you have a close connection with any organizations?
CUMMC is an agency of The United Methodist Church. CUMMC had a church charter granted to it by the California-Pacific Annual Conference of The United Methodist Church from 1968 to 2011. CUMMC reports regarding its activities and receives guidance from the Conference through the South District Superintendent and the South District Union (Trustees).

Appendix I: Lease Contract (Sample)

This LEASE AGREEMENT is entered into as of January 1, 2015, by and between Christ United Methodist Ministry Center (CMC), a California non-profit organization ("LESSOR-(CMC)") and ABC Charity (ABC), a California 501(c)(3) non-profit organization ("LESSEE-(ABC)"). This lease replaces and supersedes any and all existing leases.

SECTION 1: BASIC AGREEMENT

Leased Spaces and Times: Specifically, LESSEE-(ABC) shall have primary use of the following spaces for group support, fellowship, and addiction education:

SPACE USED	DAY(S) USED	TIME USED
Room 228	Weekdays (M-F)	8:00 a.m. – 6:00 p.m.

Minor changes to the days and times may be made only with the approval of LESSOR-(CMC)'S Director and Office Manager, provided such changes do not conflict with other LESSEE-(ABC)'S schedules. (See also 6.4 Scheduling Special Events.)

1.2 Term of Lease: The lease term shall be for nine and a half months commencing on January 1, 2015, and shall terminate on December 31, 2015. After that date, LESSEE-(ABC) shall be on a month-to-month contract at the same rate until another lease contract is in place.

1.3 Rent: The rent for the lease term shall be payable in monthly installments of One Hundred Sixty Dollars ($160.00) throughout the term of the lease.

1.4 Security Deposit: LESSOR-(CMC) waives the requirement of a security deposit.

1.5 Late Payment: Lease rentals are due on the last business day of each week.

1.6 Termination: This lease may be terminated by agreement of either party with sixty (60) days' notice. Violation of the terms of this lease may result in immediate termination.

Upon the terms and subject to the conditions hereinafter set forth, LESSOR-(CMC) leases to LESSEE-(ABC) and LESSEE-(ABC) leases from LESSOR-(CMC), the real property described herein, located at 3295 Meade Avenue, San Diego, California 92116, with floor plan and schedule appended, together with all improvements now or hereafter located thereon and all appurtenances and privileges related thereto, all of which area is hereinafter referred to as the "Premises."

The policies and terms of this contract are written to both protect the property and help ensure a positive experience for all the groups and organizations that use the Premises, whether for a single event or over a long-term contract. Every group has a responsibility to the whole community. All groups and individuals using church property must do so in a spirit of respect, care and responsibility.

SECTION 2: REQUIREMENTS

2.1 Tax Exemption and Insurance: Each group or organization contracting space at LESSOR-(CMC) must have:

- A 501(c)(3) IRS tax-exemption from the Internal Revenue Service, or other qualifying tax-exemption
- An Organization Clearance Certificate (OCC) from the California Board of Equalization
- A Welfare Exemption from the County Tax Assessor for the current year, and required timely filing annually by February 15
- Insurance Coverage:
  - At its sole cost and expense, LESSEE-(ABC) shall obtain and thereafter maintain in full force and effect, at all times during the lease term and any extension thereof, the following insurance with respect to the Premises:
  - LESSEE-(ABC) must carry $1,000,000 general liability insurance. LESSEE-(ABC) must provide LESSOR-(CMC) with a certificate of insurance that names LESSOR-(CMC) as additional insured. LESSEE-(ABC) will be required to prove continuing coverage on an annual basis.
  - If LESSEE-(ABC) has employees, the certificate must include workers comp.
  - If LESSEE-(ABC) owns a vehicle in the name of the church, charity or organization, the certificate must include vehicle liability coverage of $1,000,000.
  - LESSEE-(ABC) shall indemnify LESSOR-(CMC) for, defend LESSOR-(CMC) against, and save LESSOR-(CMC) harmless from any liability, loss, cost, injury, damage, or other expense that may occur or be claimed by or with respect to any person or property on or about the

Premises resulting from the use, misuse, occupancy, possession, or un-occupancy of the Premises by LESSEE-(ABC), its agents, employees, licensees, invitees or guests.

- o LESSOR-(CMC) shall not have any liability for any loss, cost, injury or damage to the Premises, to LESSEE-(ABC) or LESSEE-(ABC)'s employees, agents, licensees, invitees or guests or to any property of such persons.
- o LESSOR-(CMC) shall not be responsible or liable for loss or damage to the contents of any improvements on the Premises, regardless of who owns the contents and regardless of how or by whom the loss or damage is caused.
- o Each insurance policy furnished by LESSEE-(ABC) shall be issued by a responsible insurance company acceptable to LESSOR-(CMC) which company shall be authorized to do business in California. LESSEE-(ABC) shall furnish LESSOR-(CMC) with memorandum copies of such insurance policies prior to the commencement of the lease.

2.2 Lost or stolen property: LESSOR-(CMC) assumes no responsibility for lost, damaged or stolen property. Please make sure your liability insurance includes coverage for damage or loss of your furnishing, equipment or other items.

2.3 Compliance with Laws and Ordinances: LESSEE-(ABC)'S use of the Premises shall be in a lawful, safe, and proper manner. LESSEE-(ABC) shall carefully preserve, protect, control and guard the same from damage. Activities prohibited on LESSOR-(CMC)'S grounds include, but not limited to, use of alcohol (except Communion wine), tobacco or controlled substances, profanity, and any destructive or illegal behavior. If any law, ordinance, order, rule or regulation is passed or enacted by any governmental agency having jurisdiction over the Premises or LESSEE-(ABC)'S use of the same which requires LESSEE-(ABC) to modify or alter its operations or use of the Premises, this Lease shall in no way be affected and LESSEE-(ABC) shall, at its sole cost and expense, promptly comply with such law, ordinance, order, rule, or regulation.

2.4 Contacts: Groups are required to provide current contact information, including names, phone numbers and e-mail addresses of your ministers, directors and official representatives. We encourage open and regular communication.

SECTION 3: LEASE TERMS

3.1 Common Areas: Common Space is available for use by all congregations and weekday ministries by reservation on a first-come basis with seven (7) days advance written notice. When LESSEE-(ABC) wants to reserve a common space, LESSEE-(ABC) will request use of the space through the official calendar maintained by the Office Manager. Under no circumstances shall the LESSEE-(ABC) assume a common space will be available without making a reservation in the official calendar. Use of a room for twenty-four (24) or more hours per week shall be considered exclusive use and LESSOR-(CMC) shall pay prorated rent for such use of common areas.

Common Areas include, unless previously reserved:
- Evangel Room 103
- Nursery Room 105
- Upper Room 202
- Jubilee Room 207
- Library
- Social Hall/Kitchenette
- Welcome Room

3.2 Hours of Operation: The building is generally open from 8:00 AM to 9:00 PM. No services or building use shall extend beyond the 9:30 PM curfew without the approval of the LESSOR-(CMC)'s Director and Office Manager. All LESSEE-(ABC)s and their clients or members are urged to respect the neighboring homes by limiting conversations, slamming car doors, music or other noises in the parking lot.

3.3 Access: LESSOR-(CMC) shall have the right to enter the Premises at all reasonable times for the purpose of inspecting the same, and during the last month of the lease term, or any renewal or extension thereof, LESSOR-(CMC) may exhibit the same for rent; provided, however, that LESSOR-(CMC) shall not unreasonably interfere with LESSEE-(ABC)'s use of the Premises.

3.4 Keys: LESSOR-(CMC) shall keep a copy of all keys used by LESSEE-(ABC) for security and facility inspections. LESSEE-(ABC) shall not duplicate or share keys to the building or exclusive use areas without the approval of the LESSOR-(CMC). LESSEE-(ABC) shall provide LESSOR-(CMC) with a copy of keys to exclusive use areas. All keys should be signed for and returned when no longer needed or at the end of a lease. Groups having private offices are required to provide a set of keys to the

Office Manager and Sexton for emergency access, including any alarm codes, if any.

3.5 Mailbox: LESSOR-(CMC) shall provide a mailbox in the Center Office where LESSEE-(ABC) may pick up mail delivered to 3295 Meade Avenue, San Diego CA 92116.

3.6 Restrooms: LESSEE-(ABC) shall have access to the restrooms on the first and second floor.

3.7 Default: If LESSEE-(ABC) fails to pay any installment of rent or make any other required payment, or if LESSEE-(ABC) fails to observe and perform any other provision, covenant, or condition of this Lease, or if LESSEE-(ABC) abandons or vacates the Premises during the continuance of this Lease, LESSOR-(CMC) shall, as it elects, either:

- declare this Lease to be in default, in which event this Lease shall immediately cease and terminate, and LESSOR-(CMC) may possess and enjoy the Premises as though this Lease had never been made, without prejudice, to any and all rights of action when LESSOR-(CMC) may have against LESSEE-(ABC) for rent and other charges payable by LESSEE-(ABC) hereunder (both past due and future rent due LESSOR-(CMC) and past due and future charges payable by LESSEE-(ABC)), damages, or breach of covenant, in respect to which LESSEE-(ABC) shall remain and continue liable notwithstanding such termination; or
- re-let the Premises, or any part thereof, for such term or terms and on such conditions, as LESSOR-(CMC) deems appropriate for and on behalf of LESSEE-(ABC), for the highest rental reasonably attainable in the judgment of LESSOR-(CMC), which re-letting shall not be considered as a surrender or acceptance back of the Premises or a termination of this Lease, and recover from LESSEE-(ABC) any deficiency between the amount of rent and all other charges payable by LESSEE-(ABC) under this Lease and those amounts obtained from such re-letting, plus any expenses incurred by LESSOR-(CMC) in connection with such re-letting, including, without limitation, the expenses of any repairs or alterations LESSOR-(CMC) deems necessary or appropriate to make in connection with such re-letting and all sums expended for brokerage commissions and reasonable attorneys' fees, but LESSOR-(CMC) shall be under no duty to re-let the Premises; or
- declare the whole amount of the rent and other charges which would otherwise have been paid by LESSEE-(ABC) over the

balance of the lease term to be immediately due and payable, without prejudice, however, to any and all other rights of action which LESSOR-(CMC) may have against LESSEE-(ABC) for past due rent and other charges payable by LESSEE-(ABC) hereunder, damages or breach of covenant, in respect to which LESSEE-(ABC) shall remain and continue liable notwithstanding LESSOR-(CMC)'s election to proceed under this clause.

SECTION 4: UTILITIES & SERVICES

Utilities costs are very high, and continue to climb. We ask that all groups and individuals be frugal and prudent with use of lighting, heating, air conditioning and water. Please turn lights off when you leave, and make sure all faucets are tightly off and toilets are not running. Wasteful energy or water use will result in increases in rent to pay for their use.

Please report water leaks, light outages or other utility problems to the Office Manager.

4.1 Water and Electricity: This AGREEMENT includes utilities for electricity and water provided by the LESSOR-(CMC).

4.2 Telephone: LESSEE-(ABC) shall be responsible for providing their own telephone service. LESSOR-(CMC) must approve any telecom connections installed by LESSEE-(ABC).

4.3 Internet Access: LESSOR-(CMC) provides high speed Wi-Fi Internet access for LESSEE-(ABC) computers. Access to the Wi-Fi is a privilege, and LESSOR-(CMC) assumes no responsibility for maintaining connectivity to the Wi-Fi on the LESSEE-(ABC)'s computers or devices after setup. Under no circumstances should LESSEE-(ABC) install any router, hub or other networking device without approval from LESSOR-(CMC). Any and all costs for additional cabling, equipment, and/or accessories to connect said computers shall be the sole cost and responsibility of LESSEE-(ABC).

4.4 Projection Services: LESSOR-(CMC) shall provide equipment for projection of images in the main sanctuary. LESSEE-(ABC) must comply with all copyright laws in use of images, lyrics, and other materials used in its worship, education or religious activities.

4.5 Closets/Cabinets/Cupboards: LESSOR-(CMC) provides a limited number of closets, cabinets and cupboards for storage of supplies. These are available on a first come, first serve basis. Please inquire with the Office Manager about availability.

4.6 Bulletin Boards: LESSOR-(CMC) provides bulletin boards as available in the Welcome Room and hallways for use by LESSOR-(CMC)S. LESSOR-(CMC) reserves the right to regulate the number, size and content of the bulletin boards on the Premises.

4.7 Custodial Care: While LESSOR-(CMC) hires professional custodial services, we expect that groups will exercise care and mature responsibility in their use of the building and all property contained therein. Please clean up after your group has finished meeting, and store any items that have been used. If there is any damage caused by your group's activities, we expect you to report it and be willing to compensate the church. Do not bring furniture or other large items onto church property without approval. Do not litter, including the curb areas in front of the church. Unfortunately, we do have problems with things being taken and not returned. Your group will be liable for missing items if there is clear evidence of wrongdoing or negligence. Please be a watchdog for us…and you. Follow directions on all signage; it is there for a reason.

4.8 Garbage Disposal: Each church or organization is responsible for disposing of garbage in accordance to policy. The white dumpster bin is for recycle materials only (glass, plastic, cardboard) and is emptied once a week. The green dumpster bin is for all other garbage and is emptied Mondays, Wednesday and Fridays. Please make sure dumpster lids are closed and that they are not overfilled as that will result in a fine from our garbage vendor. Stacking paper plates and glasses will help conserve space. Office tenants may place their full waste baskets in the hallway for our custodial staff to empty.

4.9 Website: LESSOR-(CMC) will provide a webpage on ChristSD.com website for each church or charity that operates from LESSOR-(CMC).

4.10 Electric Sign: LESSOR-(CMC) will provide basic information for each church or charity on the LESSOR-(CMC) electronic sign on the front lawn.

4.11 Pest Control: LESSOR-(CMC) shall provide pest control for the building. Please report any pest problems to the Office Manager.

4.12 Interruption of Services: LESSOR-(CMC) does not warrant that any of the utility services above-mentioned will be free from interruptions caused by war, insurrection, civil commotion, riots, acts of God or the enemy, governmental action, lockouts, picketing (whether legal or illegal), accidents, inability of LESSOR-(CMC) to obtain fuel or supplies, or any other cause or causes beyond the reasonable control of LESSOR-(CMC). Any such interruption of service shall not be deemed an eviction or disturbance of LESSEE-(ABC)'s use and possession of the Premises, or any part thereof, or render LESSOR-(CMC) liable to LESSEE-(ABC) for damages, or relieve LESSEE-(ABC) from the performance of LESSEE-(ABC)'s obligations under this Lease. LESSOR-(CMC) shall have no responsibility or liability for the failure of any public or private utility to supply sufficient or adequate utility services to the Premises.

SECTION 5: SECURITY

5.1 Security of Premises: LESSOR-(CMC) provides 24-hour security camera surveillance. LESSEE-(ABC) shall, at the end of each day, secure all interior and exterior doors and windows. We have a large building with over 20 exterior doors and many ground level windows. We require all parties to monitor entrances in your area, and make sure that all windows and doors (including restroom windows) are locked when you leave. Be aware of any suspicious entry, and seek assistance (from the police if necessary) if there is an apparent risk of personal injury, or property damage or loss. The building alarm code is known only by LESSOR-(CMC)'S staff. If you need to be in the building when alarm is set (before 7:30 AM and after 9:30 PM), please make arrangements in advance with church office. Do not assume that someone will follow immediately behind you to do a security check and lock-up. We all need to do this for our own groups.

5.2 Supervision of Children: Children are very important people, and their safety is paramount. We ask that all groups and individuals provide responsible, qualified adult supervision of children at all times. If you cannot supervise your children, please leave them at home with a sitter. You are responsible for the conduct of your children and youth, and any property damage they may cause.

SECTION 6: POLICIES

6.1 Parking Policy: LESSEE-(ABC) shall not use the parking area or the ingress and egress area of the Premises in an unreasonable manner so as to interfere with the normal flow of traffic or the use of such areas by occupants of properties adjacent to the Premises. The parking lot is the property of the church, and all policies stated above apply, as do all traffic laws. Parking is restricted to marked stalls: Do not block through traffic in parking lot. Please back up and drive carefully, as children and the elderly are often present. Note that traffic through lot is ONE WAY from east to west only, and you must turn RIGHT onto 33rd Place (a one-way street). Be respectful of the neighbors by controlling noise level. Please park all motorcycles and over-sized vehicles on street. Dumpsters are for building use only.

6.2 Kitchen Policy: Use of the kitchen is a privilege arranged with each group through the church office. You are requested to leave the kitchen as clean as you found it, and to securely bag your trash (please furnish your own trash bags). Make sure all appliances and the stove/oven are turned off when you leave. Make sure doors are locked. Do not use food or supplies your group has not furnished. Any uneaten perishables are to be taken home or thrown out, unless there is agreement to do otherwise. DO NOT put food or coffee grounds in sinks. DO NOT leave your group's items in the kitchen without specific permission. Please coordinate any storage with the church office, and make sure everything is clearly labeled. If the kitchen is not left in good order, there will be a clean-up charge of $25 per hour for custodial clean-up fees. We request that you report any problems you discover to the church office.

IMPORTANT: NO FOOD SHOULD EVER BE CONSUMED OUTSIDE THE SOCIAL HALL!

6.3 Yard Sale Policy: According to City ordinance, we are entitled to conduct nine (9) yard sales per year. Please schedule yard sales with the Office Manager. Yard sales may be held on the front lawn, and should never use loud or amplified music to respect our neighbors.

6.4 Scheduling Special Events: Any events made outside the days and time schedule of this agreement MUST be made with the approval of the Office Manager or Director. To prevent conflicts in scheduling, DO NOT make arrangements between your group and another group without first scheduling a change or special event with the Office Manager. Without a scheduling receipt, you may not assume a space will be available. If a conflict occurs, the group with the prior scheduling receipt will have use of the space.

SECTION 7: PROHIBITED ACTIVITIES

7.1 Smoking: Our insurance policy requires that there be no smoking on church property, including lawn and parking areas. The LESSOR-(CMC) trustees also request that the surrounding sidewalks be smoke free. We urge that when you come to LESSOR-(CMC), come prepared to not smoke.

7.2 Animals: LESSOR-(CMC) does not allow animals in the building except for service animals, unless there is special permission. Please contact the church office if you have any questions (619-284-9205).

7.3 Noise: LESSEE-(ABC) shall take care to comply with all city ordinances, including but not limited to noise abatement, respecting the rights and privacy of neighbors who are located close by the church. Please keep doors and windows closed during worship to contain the volume of noise that may impact our neighbors.

SECTION 8: USE, MAINTENANCE AND REPAIR

8.1 Furniture, Fixtures, and Equipment: Other than fixed furnishings, such as church pews, pulpit, etc., LESSEE-(ABC) shall provide, keep, and maintain any and all furniture, fixtures, and equipment required to perform their activities, operations, and/or business activities. LESSOR-(CMC) shall not bear any expense for the acquisition, moving, or maintaining of LESSEE-(ABC)'s furniture, fixtures, and equipment and shall not be held responsibility for any cost of replacement for same as stated elsewhere within the confines of this AGREEMENT.

8.2 Maintenance and Repair: LESSOR-(CMC) shall, at its sole cost and expense, keep and maintain the Premises, including without limitation, the roof, exterior, foundation, structural and operational parts (cooling, heating, plumbing equipment and fixtures), paving and landscaping, interior maintenance (floors, doors, toilets, light replacement, etc.), and all other elements or systems of the Premises, in a condition and repair similar to its original condition and repair, reasonable wear and tear excepted. Replacement and repair parts, materials, and equipment used by LESSEE-(ABC) shall be of a quality equivalent to those initially installed within the Premises. All repair and maintenance will be done in accordance with the then existing federal, state, and local laws, regulations and ordinances pertaining thereto. Except as otherwise provided in Sections 11 and 12, below, LESSEE-(ABC) shall have no obligation whatsoever with respect to the maintenance and repair of the Premises, except for damage done by LESSEE-(ABC) to the premises.

8.3 Alterations and Improvements: LESSEE-(ABC) shall have the right to make, at no expense to LESSOR-(CMC), improvements, alterations, or additions (hereinafter collectively referred to as "Alteration") to the Premises, whether interior or exterior, provided that:

- no Alteration shall be made without the prior written consent of LESSOR-(CMC), which consent shall not be unreasonably withheld;
- no Alteration shall reduce or otherwise impair the value of the Premises;
- no Alteration shall be commenced until LESSEE-(ABC) has first obtained and paid for all required permits and authorizations of all governmental authorities having jurisdiction with respect to such Alteration;
- any Alteration shall be made in a good workmanlike manner and in compliance with all laws, ordinances, regulations, codes, and permits;
- LESSEE-(ABC) shall hold LESSOR-(CMC) harmless from and against any liens and claims for work, labor, or materials supplied to the Premises at the direction of LESSEE-(ABC), and in the event that any such liens or claims shall be filed for work, labor or materials supplied to the Premises at the direction of LESSEE-(ABC), LESSEE-(ABC) shall, at LESSOR-(CMC)'s option, either escrow an amount equal to the amount of the lien or claim being filed, or obtain a bond for the protection of LESSOR-(CMC) in an amount not less than the amount of the lien or claim being filed; and
- any Alteration shall become and remain the property of LESSOR-(CMC) unless LESSOR-(CMC) otherwise agrees in writing.

8.4 Signs: LESSEE-(ABC) shall have the right to install and operate, at its sole cost and expense, any sign or signs on the Premises which shall not be in violation of any law, statute or ordinance, and LESSEE-(ABC) shall have the right to remove the same, provided that LESSEE-(ABC) must repair any damage to the Premises caused by such removal. Prior to the installation of any signage on the premises, LESSOR-(CMC) shall retain the exclusive right of prior approval of said signage. LESSEE-(ABC) shall submit, in writing to LESSOR-(CMC)'s Director all requests for signage, inclusive of size, color, and location. Interior signs shall be similar in size and design as existing interior signage. LESSOR-(CMC) shall provide LESSEE-(ABC) information on the main exterior electronic sign.

8.5 Major Damage to Premises: If by fire or other casualty the Premises are destroyed or damaged to the extent that LESSEE-(ABC) is deprived of occupancy or use of the Premises (meaning such destruction cannot be repaired or restored within 120 days of the occurrence of the fire or other casualty LESSOR-(CMC) may elect to:
cause the restoration of the Premises to substantially the same condition as existed before such damage or destruction; or
cancel this Lease as of the date of such fire or casualty by giving written notice to LESSEE-(ABC) not more than 30 days thereafter.

Should LESSOR-(CMC) elect to proceed under (a), above, rent shall abate unless LESSEE-(ABC) continues to partially occupy the Premises in which case LESSEE-(ABC) shall pay all rent on a prorated basis, until the Premises are restored, equal to an amount obtained by multiplying the then existing monthly rent by a percentage equal to the fraction which has as its numerator the amount of square feet in the improvements of the Premises which is incapable of being used for its intended purpose and as its denominator the total amount of square feet in the improvements on the premises. If such damage does not deprive LESSEE-(ABC) of occupancy or use of the Premises, LESSOR-(CMC) shall proceed with due diligence to cause the restoration of the Premises to substantially the same condition as existed before such damage. In such latter event, rent shall not abate. LESSEE-(ABC) shall fully cooperate with LESSOR-(CMC) in making available to LESSOR-(CMC) for the purpose of so restoring the Premises all insurance proceeds payable under Section 8 as a result of fire or other casualty damage to the Premises.

SECTION 9: EXCLUSIONS

9.1 Condemnation: If all or materially all of the Premises are taken in appropriation proceedings or by right of eminent domain or by the threat of the same, then this Lease shall terminate as of the date LESSEE-(ABC) is deprived of occupancy thereof, and LESSEE-(ABC)'s obligations under this Lease, except obligations for rent and other charges herein to be paid by LESSEE-(ABC) up to the date thereof, shall terminate. For purposes of this Lease, "materially all of the Premises" shall be considered as having been taken if the portion of the Premises taken, due either to the area so taken or the location of the portion taken, would leave the remaining portion not so taken insufficient to enable LESSEE-(ABC) to effectively and economically conduct it business at the Premises.

9.2 Non-Waiver and Right to Cure Defaults: Neither a failure by LESSOR-(CMC) to exercise any of its options hereunder, nor a failure to enforce its rights or seek its remedies upon any default, nor an acceptance by LESSOR-(CMC) of any rent accruing before or after any default, shall affect or constitute a waiver of LESSOR-(CMC)'s right to exercise such option, to enforce such right, or to seek such remedy with respect to that default or to any prior or subsequent default. The remedies provided in this Lease shall be cumulative and shall not in any way abridge, modify or preclude any other rights or remedies to which LESSOR-(CMC) is entitled, either at law or in equity.

9.3 Estoppel Certificate: LESSEE-(ABC) shall, at LESSOR-(CMC)'s request upon not less than ten days' prior notice by LESSOR-(CMC), execute, acknowledge, and deliver to LESSOR-(CMC), or such other party as LESSOR-(CMC) may specify, a statement in writing certifying that this Lease has not been modified and is still in full force and effect (or if modified, that the same is in full force and effect as modified and stating the modifications), and the dates to which the rent and any other obligations to be paid hereunder by LESSEE-(ABC) have been paid, and stating whether or not, to the best of the knowledge of LESSEE-(ABC), LESSEE-(ABC) or LESSOR-(CMC) is in default in performance of any obligation hereunder, and if so, specifying each such default.

9.4 Holding Over by LESSEE-(ABC): If LESSEE-(ABC) shall continue in possession of the Premises beyond the termination of the lease term, such holding over shall be considered an extension of this Lease for a one-month period and so on, from month to month, until terminated by either party by giving not less than 30 days written notice of termination to the other. Such holding over shall be upon the same terms and conditions as are set forth in this Lease.

9.5 Surrender of Premises: Upon termination of this Lease, whether by lapse of time or otherwise, or upon the exercise by LESSOR-(CMC) of the power to enter and repossess the Premises without terminating this Lease, as hereinbefore provided, LESSEE-(ABC) shall at once surrender possession of the Premises to LESSOR-(CMC) in a condition and order of repair substantially similar to its original condition and order of repair upon the commencement of the lease term, reasonable wear and tear and damage, and shall at once remove all of LESSEE-(ABC)'s personal property and trade fixtures from the Premises. Upon any such termination, LESSEE-(ABC) shall, as directed by LESSOR-(CMC), either remodel any addition to the Premises constructed by LESSEE-(ABC) so as to facilitate use of such addition for office operations or remove such addition from the Premises. Any such remodeling or removal of any addition to the Premises shall be made by LESSEE-(ABC) at its sole cost and expense. If, upon any such termination, LESSEE-(ABC) does not at once surrender possession of the Premises and remove such of its property as allowed by LESSOR-(CMC), LESSOR-(CMC) may forthwith re-enter and repossess the same and remove all of LESSEE-(ABC)'s property without being guilty of trespass or of forceful entry or detainer or without incurring any liability to LESSEE-(ABC) for loss or damage to LESSEE-(ABC)'s property. Upon any such removal of LESSEE-(ABC)'s property, it shall be considered to have been abandoned and may either be retained by LESSOR-(CMC) as its property or may be disposed of at public or private sale as LESSOR-(CMC) sees fit. If any such property is either sold at public or private sale or retained by LESSOR-(CMC), the proceeds of any such sale or the then current fair market value of the property, as the case may be, shall be applied by LESSOR-(CMC) against LESSOR-(CMC)'s expenses of removal, storage or sale of such property, the arrears of rent and other charges or future rent and other charges payable hereunder, and any other damages to which LESSOR-(CMC) may be entitled hereunder. LESSEE-(ABC) shall repair, at its sole cost and expense, any damage to the Premises resulting from the removal of its property as allowed hereunder.

9.6 Time of the Essence: Time is of the essence in the performance and observance of each and every term, covenant and condition of this Lease by both LESSOR-(CMC) and LESSEE-(ABC).

9.7 Assignment: LESSEE-(ABC) shall not assign this Lease or sublet the Premises, or any part thereof, without the prior written consent of LESSOR-(CMC), which consent may be subject to terms and conditions as LESSOR-(CMC) considers necessary in order to protect its interest in the premises; provided, however, that no assignment of this Lease, whether by act of LESSEE-(ABC) or by operation of law, and no sublease of the premises, or any part thereof, by or from LESSEE-(ABC), shall relieve or release LESSEE-(ABC) from any of its obligations hereunder.

9.8 Governing Law: This Lease shall be subject to and governed by the laws of the State of California even though one or more of the parties may be or may become a resident of a different state.

9.9 Amendments: No amendment to this Lease shall be valid or binding unless such amendment is in writing and executed by the parties hereto.

9.10 Severability of Provisions: The invalidity or unenforceability of any particular provision of this Lease shall not affect the other provisions hereof and this Lease shall be construed in all respects as if such invalid or unenforceable provision were omitted.

IN WITNESS WHEREOF, LESSOR-(CMC) and LESSEE-(ABC) have executed this Lease AGREEMENT as of the date first set forth above. Signed and acknowledged

LESSOR-(CMC):

_____   _____
Signed   Date

LESSEE-(ABC):

_____   _____
Signed   Date

Appendix J: Building Use Policy Sample

The following are the policies adopted by the Board of Trustees of Christ United Methodist Ministry Center (CUMMC). These policies are to be followed by all groups or individuals using the church building. Please read carefully, and review with your members.

I General: The properties of CUMMC, including its parking and landscaped areas, are dedicated for worship, Christian education and related ministries. All groups and individuals using church property need to do so in a spirit of respect, propriety and goodwill. Activities prohibited on church grounds include use of alcohol, tobacco or controlled substances, profanity, and any destructive or illegal behavior. We do not allow animals in the building except for service animals, unless there is special permission. Please contact the church office if you have any questions (619-284-9205).

II Requirements for Groups: Any group or organization contracting space at CUMMC must have a 501(c)(3) filed with the County Tax Assessor's Office and the CUMMC office. Annual filings will be required by the Assessor's Office. All groups are required to carry liability insurance of no less than $1,000,000.

III Security: We have a large building with over 20 exterior doors and many ground level windows. We require all parties to monitor entrances in your area, and make sure that all windows and doors (including restroom windows) are locked when you leave. Be aware of any suspicious entry, and seek assistance (from the police if necessary) if there is an apparent risk of personal injury, or property damage or loss. If you are issued keys, DO NOT have copies made, or share them with others. The building alarm code is known only by staff and trustees. If you need to be in the building when alarm is set (before 7:30 AM and after 9:30 PM), please make arrangements in advance with church office. All keys should be signed for and returned when no longer needed. Do not assume that someone will follow immediately behind you to do a security check and lock-up. We all need to do this for our own groups. Groups having private offices are required to give a set of keys to the trustees for emergency access, including any alarm codes. CUMMC is not responsible for any loss or damage to items brought to the church by your group or members of your group.

IV Energy and Water Use: Our utilities costs are very high, and continue to climb. We ask that all groups and individuals be frugal and prudent with use of lighting, heating, air conditioning and water. Please turn lights off when you leave, and make sure all faucets are tightly off and toilets are not running. If you are wasteful in energy or water use, we will ask for a fair compensation.

V Property Care: While the church does hire professional custodial services, we expect that groups will exercise care and mature responsibility in their use of the building and all property contained therein. Please clean up after your group has finished meeting, and store any items that have been used. If there is any damage caused by your group's activities, we expect you to report it and be willing to compensate the church. Do not bring furniture or other large items onto church property without clearing it with the trustees. Do not litter, including the curb areas in front of the church. Unfortunately, we do have problems with things being taken and not returned. Your group will be liable for missing items if there is clear evidence of wrongdoing or negligence. Please be a watchdog for us…and yourselves. Follow directions on all signage; it is there for a reason.

VI Smoking: Our insurance policy requires that there be no smoking on church property, including lawn and parking areas. The CUMMC trustees also request that the surrounding sidewalks be smoke free. We urge that when you come to CUMMC, come prepared to not smoke.

VII Supervision of Children: Children are very important people, and their safety is paramount. We ask that all groups and individuals provide responsible, qualified adult supervision of children at all times. If you cannot supervise your children, please leave them at home with a sitter. You are responsible for the conduct of your children and youth, and any property damage they may cause.

VIII Kitchen: Use of the kitchen is a privilege arranged with each group through the church office. You are requested to leave the kitchen as clean as you found it, and to securely bag your trash (please furnish your own trash bags). Make sure all appliances and the stove/oven are turned off when you leave. Make sure doors (including the sliding serving window) are locked. Do not use food or supplies your group has not furnished. Any uneaten perishables are to be taken home or thrown out, unless there is agreement to do otherwise. DO NOT put food or coffee grounds in sinks or the garbage disposal. DO NOT leave your group's items in the kitchen without specific permission. Please coordinate any storage with the church office, and make sure everything is clearly labeled. If the kitchen is not left in good order, there will be a clean-up charge of $25 per hour for custodial clean-up fees. We request that you report any problems you discover to the church office.

IX Parking Lot: The parking lot is the property of the church, and all policies stated above apply, as do all traffic laws. Parking is restricted to marked stalls: Do not block through traffic in parking lot. Please back up and drive carefully, as children and the elderly are often present. Note that traffic through lot is from east to west only, and you must turn RIGHT onto 33rd Place (a one-way street). Be respectful of the neighbors by controlling noise level. Please park all motorcycles and over-sized vehicles on street. Dumpsters are for building use only. Make sure dumpster lids are closed.

X Compensation: Arrangements for monthly payments are made with each group. Honor these commitments by paying promptly at the first of each month, and making payments in full. Please contact the church office with any questions about payments. Non-payment will result in eviction.

XI Contacts: Groups are requested to provide current contact information to the trustees, including names, phone numbers and e-mail addresses of your official representatives. We encourage open and regular communication.

These policies are written to both protect the property and help ensure a positive experience for all the groups and organizations that use the building, whether for a single event or over a long-term contract. Think of the church as a mission center, where every group has a role and responsibility to the whole community.

Use Policy Signed:

_____   _____
Name of Organization   Church or Organization Contact

_____   _____
Title   Date

Appendix K: Director's Job Description

The Executive Director is responsible for the successful leadership and management of the organization according to the strategic direction set by the Board of Directors. Due to the unique nature of Christ Ministry Center, the Executive Director must have a combination of knowledge, skills, and experience in both United Methodist polity and procedures defined in The Book of Discipline, and legal guidelines for Non-Profit Management, including city, state, federal and IRS regulations.

Primary Duties and Responsibilities
The Executive Director fulfills the following roles and performs the following tasks:

Leadership
- Participates with the Board of Directors in developing a vision and strategic plan to guide the organization
- Identifies, assesses, and informs the Board of Directors of internal and external issues that affect the organization
- Acts as a professional advisor to the Board of Director on all aspects of the organization's activities
- Fosters effective team work between the Board and the Executive Director and between the Executive Director and staff
- In addition to the Chair of the Board, acts as a spokesperson for the organization
- Conducts official correspondence on behalf of the Board as appropriate and jointly with the Board when appropriate
- Represents the organization at community activities to enhance the organization's community profile

Operational planning and management
- Develops an operational plan which incorporates goals and objectives that work towards the strategic direction of the organization
- Ensures that the operation of the organization meets the expectations of its clients, Board, Donors and The United Methodist Church
- Oversees the efficient and effective day-to-day operation of the organization
- Drafts policies for the approval of the Board and prepares procedures to implement the organizational policies; reviews

existing policies on an annual basis and recommends changes to the Board as appropriate
- Ensures that personnel, client, donor and volunteer files are securely stored and privacy/confidentiality is maintained
- Provides support to the Board by preparing meeting agenda and supporting materials

Program planning and management
- Oversees the planning, implementation and evaluation of the organization's programs and services
- Ensures that the programs and services offered by the organization contribute to the organization's mission and reflect the priorities of the Board
- Monitors the day-to-day delivery of the programs and services of the organization to maintain or improve quality
- Oversees the planning, implementation, execution and evaluation of special projects

Human resources planning and management
- Determines staffing requirements for organizational management and program delivery
- Oversees the implementation of the human resources policies, procedures and practices including the development of job description for all staff
- Establishes a positive, healthy and safe work environment in accordance with all appropriate legislation and regulations
- Recruits, interviews and selects staff that have the right technical and personal abilities to help further the organization's mission
- Ensures that all staff receives an orientation to the organization and provides appropriate training
- Implements a performance management process for all staff which includes monitoring the performance of staff on an on-going basis and conducting an annual performance review
- Coaches and mentors staff as appropriate to improve performance
- Disciplines staff when necessary using appropriate techniques; releases staff when necessary using appropriate and legally defensible procedures

Financial planning and management
- Works with staff and the Board (Finance Committee) to prepare a comprehensive budget

- Works with the Board to secure adequate funding for the operation of the organization
- Researches funding sources, oversees the development of fund raising plans and writes funding proposals to increase the funds of the organization
- Participates in fundraising activities as appropriate
- Approves expenditures within the authority delegated by the Board
- Ensures that sound bookkeeping and accounting procedures are followed
- Administers the funds of the organization according to the approved budget and monitor the monthly cash flow of the organization
- Provides the Board with comprehensive, regular reports on the revenues and expenditure of the organization
- Ensures that the organization complies with all legislation covering taxation and withholding payments

Community relations/advocacy
- Communicates with stakeholders to keep them informed of the work of the organization and to identify changes in the community served by the organization
- Establishes good working relationships and collaborative arrangements with community groups, funders, government leaders, and other organizations to help achieve the goals of the organization

Risk management
- Identifies and evaluates the risks to the organization's people (clients, staff, management, volunteers), property, finances, goodwill, and image and implements measures to control risks
- Ensures that the Board of Directors and the organization carries appropriate and adequate insurance coverage
- Ensures that the Board and staff understand the terms, conditions and limitations of the insurance coverage

Qualifications
- Education: Accredited college degree, Master's degree preferred
- Professional designation: Ordained clergy with entrepreneurial skills and/or Non-Profit Business Administrator preferred

Knowledge, skills and abilities
- Knowledge of leadership and management principles of non-profit/ voluntary organizations
- Knowledge of all federal and provincial legislation applicable to voluntary sector organizations including: employment standards, human rights, occupational health and safety, charities, taxation, health coverage etc.
- Knowledge of current community challenges and opportunities relating to the mission of the organization
- Knowledge of human resources management
- Knowledge of financial management
- Knowledge of project management
- Proficiency in the use of computers for:
- Word processing, Spreadsheets, E-mail

Personal characteristics
The Executive Director should demonstrate competence in some or all of the following:
- Adaptability: Demonstrates a willingness to be flexible, versatile and/or tolerant in a changing work environment while maintaining effectiveness and efficiency.
- Behave Ethically, Integrity: Understands ethical behavior and business practices, and ensure that own behavior and the behavior of others is consistent with these standards and aligns with the values of the organization.
- Build Relationships: Establishes and maintains positive working relationships with others, both internally and externally, to achieve the goals of the organization.
- Communicate Effectively: Speaks, listens and writes in a clear, thorough and timely manner using appropriate and effective communication tools and techniques.
- Creativity/Innovation: Develops new and unique ways to improve operations of the organization and to create new opportunities.
- Focus on Client Needs: Anticipates, understands, and responds to the needs of internal and external clients to meet or exceed their expectations within the organizational parameters.
- Foster Teamwork: Works cooperatively and effectively with others to set goals, resolve problems, and make decisions that enhance organizational effectiveness.
- Lead: Positively influence others to achieve results that are in the best interest of the organization.

- Make Decisions: Assesses situations to determine the importance, urgency and risks, and makes clear decisions which are timely and in the best interests of the organization.
- Organize: Sets priorities, develops a work schedule, monitors progress towards goals, and tracks details, data, information and activities
- Plan: Determines strategies to move the organization forward, sets goals, creates and implements actions plans, and evaluates the process and results.
- Solve Problems: Assesses problem situations to identify causes, gathers and processes relevant information, generates possible solutions, and makes recommendations and/or resolves the problem.
- Think Strategically: Assesses options and actions based on trends and conditions in the environment, and the vision and values of the organization.

Experience
5 or more years of progressive management experience in a voluntary sector organization.
(Adapted from HRCouncil.ca)

Appendix L: Strategic and other Decisions Checklist

#	Question	Chapter	Decision
1. Organization/Function			
1a	What is the name for the new organization?	17	
1b	What is your new mission (purpose) statement?	14,17&21	
1c	What is your new business model? *(how you are going to function)*	12	
1d	How are you going to generate revenue?	12	
1d1	Are you going to rent space to charities?	21	
1d1a	- Are there any restrictions on the types of charities?	21	
1d2	Are you going to rent space to churches?	21	
1d2a	- Are there any restrictions on the types of churches?	21	
1d3	Are you going to rent space to other organizations or businesses?	21	
1d3a	- Are there any restrictions on the types of orgs/businesses?	21	
1e	How are you going to handle your legacy congregation?	21	
1f	What are your future staff positions?	21	
1fa	- Will you transition any of your existing staff to the new positions?	21	
1g	What will you do about any existing tenants?	21	
2. Facilities			
2a	How will you address facility shortfalls identified in the facility assessment?	21	
2b	How will you mitigate risks identified in the facility assessment?	21	
2c	How will you finance facility repairs & improvements for new model?	21	
3. Legal			
3a	How are you going to be organized as far as a corporation?	17	

3b	Are you going to be a new corporation or amend your current articles?	**17**	
3c	Are you going to be a member or non-member organization?	**17**	
3d	Are you going to directly or indirectly serve people?	**17**	
3e	Do you need an attorney to file forms with the Secretary of State or IRS?	**17**	
3f	Who will be on your Board?	**17**	
3g	How will you handle any existing contracts (service or rentals)?	**17**	
4. General			
4a	How have you planned to manage your technology & website transition?	**26**	
4b	Are you going to outsource any of your service needs? *(payroll, bill paying, security, waste management, pest control, etc.)*	**17**	
4c	How will the new organization handle any existing debt?	**21**	
4d	Are you going to need additional or different banking?	**21**	

Appendix M: Ministry Center Organization Model

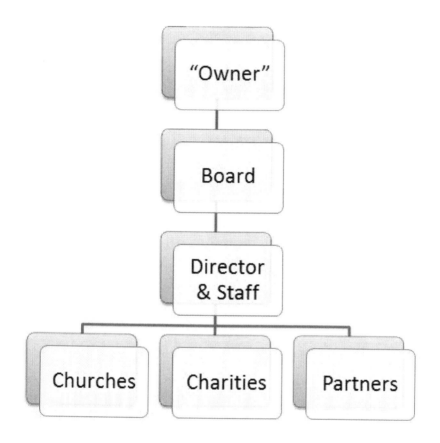

Appendix N: Revenue Stream Model

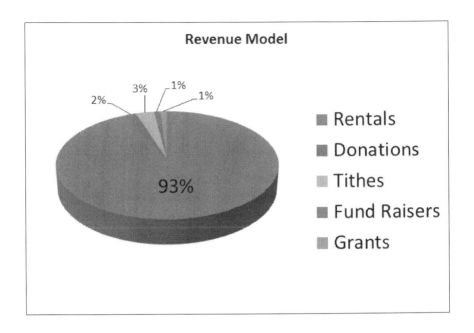

Appendix O: Memorandum of Understanding (MOU) Sample

MEMORANDUM OF UNDERSTANDING AND AGREEMENT BETWEEN CHRIST UNITED METHODIST MINISTRY CENTER AND ABC CHARITY

INTRODUCTION

THIS MEMORANDUM OF AGREEMENT ("Memorandum"), dated May 19, 2015 between CHRIST UNITED METHODIST MINISTRY CENTER ("CHRIST MINISTRY CENTER") an ecumenical, non-profit corporation established under the laws of the State of California with its offices in 3295 Meade Avenue, San Diego, California, represented by Rev. Dr. Bill Jenkins, President and Director, and ABC CHARITY, a California non-profit corporation with its principal place of business in San Diego, California, represented by Dr. John Doe, CEO and Founder; collectively referred to as "the Partners".

PREAMBLES

WHEREAS, CHRIST UNITED METHODIST MINISTRY CENTER is a non-profit organization qualified under Section 501(c)(3) of the United States Internal Revenue Code, established with the goal of assisting non-profit charities and churches in the San Diego area in such a way that enables them to be more efficient and effective in helping the helpless; particularly, the hungry, spiritually thirsty, unclothed, sick, imprisoned and strangers.

WHEREAS, ABC CHARITY is a non-profit organization, qualified under Section 501(c)(3) of the United States Internal Revenue Code and organized for the purposes of the delivery of services for ex-offenders and is recognized for social service, peer support, and referral for medical, mental health, housing, peer support, and substance abuse problems is ready, willing, and able to provide such services.

WHEREAS, this Agreement has as its objective the collaboration and participation of both organizations for the re-entry of incarcerated females into the community in such a way that reduces recidivism in the penal system and helps these women get a positive re-entry into the community.

WHEREAS, the missions of the Partners are complementary;

THEREFORE, the Partners wish to continue working together and in compliance with the following clauses:

GOAL

The primary goal of this agreement is to provide a one-stop, first stop re-entry center for female inmates upon release from jail in San Diego County.

AREAS OF COLLABORATION

The combination of ABC Charity's long and distinguished history of providing social services, peer support, referral for medical, mental health, housing, and substance abuse problems, among other services, and Christ Ministry Center's network of churches, charities and social agencies providing the essential resources these women need upon re-entry will help reach the Partners achieve the goal.

RESPONSIBILITIES OF ABC CHARITY

Services to be provided by ABC Charity to women inmates being released from the San Diego County Sheriff's Department shall include the following:

- Provide referrals for assistance upon release, including Mental Health Services, Substance Abuse Rehabilitation, Health Services, including medical and dental care, Housing and other community programs and services as may be needed.
- Provide linkages to emergency and supportive services, including, but not limited to:
- Social services
- Peer support
- Referral for medical and mental health services
- Housing assistance
- Substance abuse problems counseling and support
- Education, job skills training and career development
- Provide focus groups to present program education and begin client engagement.
- Provide in-custody pre-release needs assessments and re-entry planning.

RESPONSIBILITIES OF CHRIST MINISTRY CENTER

Christ Ministry Center will provide through its network of onsite and offsite congregations, charities, and social agencies such basic necessities as food, clothing, shelter, employment and job training, transportation, wellness services, counseling, etc.

Christ Ministry Center will provide:
- Office space for ABC Charity's staff
- Onsite food pantry and clothes closet
- Emergency temporary shelter space
- Spiritual counselors

Additional connections with other agencies through Christ Ministry Center's Fount of Blessings Ministry (MyFount.com) who provide the following services for: Addiction & Recovery, Children, Domestic Abuse, Education & Training, Employment & Career, Financial assistance, Human Trafficking, Immigration & Refugees, Justice & Human Rights, Legal, Literacy, Mental Health, Military & Families, Social Services, Thrift Shops, Transportation, Veterans.

INSURANCE

General Liability. ABC Charity shall maintain at all times an insurance policy from a reputable and licensed carrier and will name Christ Ministry Center as an additional insured against loss from any personal liability or property damage arising from any operation or activity of Welcome Home Ministries, its agents, or employees as provided for in this Agreement.

CONFIDENTIALITY

ABC Charity acknowledges that data, and referral information is sensitive and shall treat all such data and information as confidential and shall exercise the standard care to protect the confidential and proprietary data. Welcome Home Ministries further agrees to abide by all Federal and California state laws requiring confidentiality of records.

ORAL REPRESENTATION

It is specifically understood and agreed hereby that this MOU contains the complete expression of the whole Agreement between the parties hereto, and that there are no promises, representations, agreements, warranties, or inducements, either expressed or implied by said parties, except as are set forth herein; and further, that this Agreement cannot be enlarged, modified, or changed in any respect except by written agreement duly executed by and between the said parties.

Time is of the essence of this agreement and each and all of its provisions.

The waiver by Christ Ministry Center of any breach of any term, covenant, or condition herein contained shall not be deemed to be a waiver of any subsequent breach of the same or any other term, covenant, or condition herein contained.

TERM OF AGREEMENT

The term of this Agreement shall begin January 1, 2015, and continue to such time as either party gives 30 days' notice of its desire to terminate the agreement.

PRINCIPAL CONTACTS

The Principal Contacts for each one of the organizations is:

CHRIST UNITED METHODIST MINISTRY CENTER
     Rev. Dr. Bill Jenkins
     President and Director
     3295 Meade Ave, San Diego CA 92116
     (619) 723-1371 mobile (619) 284-9205 office

ABC CHARITY
     Dr. John Doe
     1234 First Street
     San Diego CA 92101
     (619) 555-1212

Such Principal Contacts may be changed in writing from time to time by their respective Partners.

USE OF INTELLECTUAL PROPERTY

The parties agree that any intellectual property, which is jointly developed through activities covered under this MOU, can be used by either party for non-profit, non-commercial purposes without obtaining consent from the other and without any need to account to the other.

All other intellectual property used in the implementation of the MOU will remain the property of the party that provided it.

An exception: intellectual property developed for The Fount of Blessings, is owned by Vandor LLC. This property can be used by either party for purposes covered by the MOU but consent will be obtained from the owner of the property before using it for purposes not covered by the MOU.

EFFECTIVE DATES AND AMENDMENTS.

This MOU shall take effect upon signing by both Parties and shall remain in effect until terminated by either or both Partners with 30 days' notice. Neither party may assign or transfer all or any portion of this MOU without the prior written consent of the other party.

The MOU may be revised by mutual written agreement by both Parties. The provisions of this MOU may only be amended or waived by mutual written agreement by both Parties. Any Party may terminate this MOU and any related agreement, work plan and budget at any time and for any reason by giving thirty (30) days prior written notice to the other Party.

The individuals signing this MOU on behalf of their respective entities represent and warrant (without personal liability therefor) that upon the signature of each, this MOU shall have been duly executed by the entity each represents.

TRANSFER OF FUNDS.

The parties acknowledge and agree that this MOU does not create any financial or funding obligation on either party, and that such obligations shall arise only upon joint execution of a subsequent agreement, contract or work plan (which shall include a budget) that specifically delineates the terms and nature of such obligations and that references this MOU. Such subsequent agreements or work plans, and budgets, will be subject to funding being specifically available for the purposes outlined therein. All PARTNER funds are further subject to PARTNER's obligation to expend PARTNER funds solely in accordance with the agreed upon budget and the line items contained therein.

NO JOINT VENTURE

Notwithstanding the terms "Partners" and "Partnership", the Partners agree that they are not entering into a Legal Partnership, joint venture or other such business arrangement, nor is the purpose of the Partners to enter into a commercial undertaking for monetary gain. Neither Partner will refer to or treat the arrangements under this Agreement as a Legal Partnership or take any action inconsistent with such intention.

DISPUTE RESOLUTION

The Partners hereby agree that, in the event of any dispute between the Partners relating to this Agreement, the Partners shall first seek to resolve the dispute through informal discussions. In the event any dispute cannot be resolved informally within sixty (60) calendar and consecutive days, the

Partners agree that the dispute will be negotiated between the Partners through mediation, if Partners can agree on a mediator. The costs of mediation shall be shared equally by the Partners. Neither Partner waives its legal rights to adjudicate this Agreement in a legal forum.

ENTIRETY

This Agreement, including all Annexes, embodies the entire and complete understanding and agreement between the Partners and no amendment will be effective unless signed by both Partners. Such signature by both Partners may be made by fax.

FOR: CHRIST MINISTRY CENTER   FOR: ABC CHARITY

_____   _____

William L. Jenkins   Dr. John Doe
President and Director   ABC Charity Founder &
CEO

Date: Date:

Appendix P: Scheduling Sample

	SUNDAY			
	SANCTUARY	**CHAPEL**	**SOCIAL HALL**	**EVANGEL RM**
6:00 AM	Ethiopian Orthodox	Open	Open	Open
7:00 AM	Ethiopian Orthodox	Open	Open	Open
8:00 AM	Ethiopian Orthodox	Open	Exodus UMC	Exodus UMC
9:00 AM	Ethiopian Orthodox	Open	Exodus UMC	Exodus UMC
10:00 AM	Exodus UMC	Christ Chapel	Exodus UMC	Exodus UMC
11:00 AM	Exodus UMC	Christ Chapel	Open	Be Encouraged
12:00 PM	Exodus UMC	Christ Chapel	New Jerusalem	Be Encouraged
1:00 PM	Ministerio Hispano	Be Encouraged	New Jerusalem	Open
2:00 PM	Ministerio Hispano	Be Encouraged	New Jerusalem	Open
3:00 PM	Ministerio Hispano	Marshallese Church	New Jerusalem	Open
4:00 PM	Open	Marshallese Church	Open	Open
5:00 PM	Open	Eritrean Church	Marshallese Church	Open
6:00 PM	Haitian Ministry	Eritrean Church	Marshallese Church	Open
7:00 PM	Haitian Ministry	Eritrean Church	Eritrean Church	Open
8:00 PM	Haitian Ministry	Eritrean	Eritrean Church	Open

Individuals and Works Cited

1. Aderhold, Rev. Dr. J. Don (Prologue) Pastor, Columbia Drive Baptist Church, Decatur GA. (1925-2013)
2. Baker, Rex (Chapter 9) Executive Director, Gateway Rescue Mission, Jackson MS
3. Bakke, Dr. Raymond J. (Chapters 8, 11) Urban Ministry Pioneer, Seattle WA, Author, "A Theology as Big as the City", InterVarsity Press, Downers Grove, IL, (1997)
4. Bennis, Warren (Chapter 19) scholar, organizational consultant and author, widely regarded as a pioneer of the contemporary field of leadership.
5. Birch, Dr. Bruce (Chapter 12) Dean, Wesley Theological Seminary, Washington DC
6. Bloom, Linda (Chapter 30) "Officially closed, but open to new ministry", United Methodist News Service, New York NY (Aug. 27, 2014)
7. Book of Discipline, The United Methodist Church, (2012)
8. Burns, Robert (Chapter 13) Scottish poet and lyricist. (1759-1796)
9. California Pacific Annual Conference, Daily Proceedings (June 2011)
10. Carcaño, Bishop Minerva (Chapter 28) Bishop, California Pacific Conference, The United Methodist Church, Pasadena CA, (2013-present)
11. Carey, William (Chapter 23) Baptist preacher and Missionary, "The father of modern missions" (1761-1834).
12. Cleveland, Donna (Chapter 9) Women's Prison and Re-entry, Welcome Home Ministries, Oceanside CA
13. Covey, Stephen (Chapter 13) Author, "7 Habits of Highly Effective People" Mango Media Inc., (June 20, 2015)
14. Crumm, Rusty (Chapter 23) Vocational Specialist at San Diego Community College District, San Diego CA
15. Darois, Ken (Chapter 27) Senior Database Developer
16. Diamandis, Peter (Chapter 10) Visionary and Author, "Abundance: The Future is Better Than You Think" Free Press; Reprint edition (September 23, 2014)
17. DiGiorgio, Linda (Chapter 10) Founder and CEO of Crossroads Ministries, Food Ministry, San Diego CA
18. Edgar, Rev. John (Chapter 10) Pastor and Director Church and Community Development for All People in Columbus OH
19. Emerson, Ralph Waldo (Chapter 15) American essayist, lecturer, and poet (1803-1882)

20. Farley, Rev. John (Chapter 30) District Superintendent, South District UMC San Diego CA
21. Francisco, Dr. Clyde T. (Chapter 11) Old Testament Seminary Professor, Southern Baptist Theological Seminary, Louisville KY and Author (1916-1981)
22. Jakes, Bishop T.D. (Chapter 14) Founder, The Potters House, Church of God in Christ (COGIC)
23. Kolender, Sheriff Bill (Chapter 9) Sheriff San Diego County CA
24. Kotler, Steven (Chapter 10) Co-author, "Abundance: The Future is Better Than You Think" Free Press; Reprint edition (September 23, 2014)
25. Lemonis, Marcus (Chapter 7) Entrepreneur, inventor, philanthropist, and television personality, CNBC "The Profit", a reality show about saving small businesses.
26. Marshall, Rev. Dr. Peter (Chapter 12) Chaplain, US Senate, Pastor, New York Avenue Presbyterian Church, Washington DC (1902-1949)
27. Meadors, Bishop Marshall (Chapter 23) Bishop, The United Methodist Church
28. Meland, Christa (Chapter 10) "Focus on assets to create positive change" Director of Communications, the Minnesota Annual Conference of the United Methodist Church, (October 8, 2015)
29. Nancarro, Maggie (Chapter 9) "The Church is not dying. The Church is failing, and there is a difference", Blogger, Director of Youth and Family Ministry & Director of Communications Twin Cities MN (June 13, 2015, www.maggienancarrow.com)
30. Oates, Rev. Dr. Wayne (Chapter 11) Professor, Southern Baptist Theological Seminary, Louisville KY, Pioneer of Modern Pastoral Care (1917-1999)
31. Parker, Richard (Chapter 19) author, author of "Lone Star Nation: How Texas Will Transform America" Pegasus; 1st edition (November 4, 2014)
32. Ramsey, Dave (Chapter 6) Christian Financial Advisor, Nashville TN
33. Roberts, David (Chapter 10) Author's childhood "best friend"
34. Sandlin, Rev. Mark (Chapter 2) Presbyterian minister, Greensboro NC
35. Shirley, Rev. Harold A. (Chapter 26) Baptist Minister. First Baptist Church, Yazoo City MS
36. Stanford, Rev. Dr. Shane (Prologue) Senior Minister and Lead Teaching Pastor of Christ United Methodist Church, Memphis TN
37. Stowers, Mark (Chapter 9) Journalist, Clarion-Ledger, Jackson MS

38. Swenson, Bishop Mary Ann (Chapters 8, 30) Bishop, California Pacific Conference, The United Methodist Church, 2004-2012
39. The Message (Paraphrase edition of The Bible)
40. United Methodist Communications (Chapter 3)
41. Warner-Robbins, Rev. Carmen (Chapter 9) MSN, RN, M.Div., FAAN, Chaplain, American Jail Association, Founder and CEO, Welcome Home Ministries, re-entry ministry for incarcerated women.
42. Weems, Rev. Dr. Lovett (Chapter 19) Distinguished Professor of Church Leadership and Director, Lewis Center for Church Leadership, Wesley Theological Seminary, Washington DC, www.churchleadership.com, (November 4, 2015)
43. Wesley, John (Prologue, Chapters 4, 8, 9, 15, 30) Founder of the Methodist church movement. (1703-1791)
44. Wingfield, Rev. Myron (Chapter 30) District Superintendent, South District, San Diego, CA California Pacific Annual Conference, The United Methodist Church

32440912R00141

Made in the USA
San Bernardino, CA
05 April 2016